MASTERING THE MESSAGE

A Practical Approach to Modern Public Relations

A must-read for PR students
and professionals alike

GANAPATHY VISWANATHAN

BlueRoseONE.com
Stories Matter
NewDelhi • London

BLUEROSE PUBLISHERS
India | U.K.

For permissions requests or inquiries regarding this publication, please contact:

BLUEROSE PUBLISHERS
www.BlueRoseONE.com
info@bluerosepublishers.com
+91 8882 898 898
+4407342408967

ISBN: 978-93-7139-808-4

Cover Design: Shubham Verma
Typesetting: Sagar

First Edition: August 2025

Introduction

Having tracked the Public Relations (PR) industry since the mid-1980s, I have witnessed its transformation from a little-understood concept to a vital strategic function. My first meaningful exposure to PR in India was at the World PR Congress in Mumbai—an event that marked a turning point for the profession in the country. The presence of Mr. Sam Black, widely regarded as the father of modern PR, was especially significant. His insights brought clarity to a profession still struggling to define itself in India.

In those early years, PR lacked structure, purpose, and credibility. Clients were sceptical, often viewing PR as secondary to advertising. The value of credibility, trust, and long-term relationship building—hallmarks of good PR—was not fully appreciated in a media environment dominated by traditional advertising.

The liberalization of the Indian economy in the 1990s, however, changed the game. As competition increased and brands sought to build lasting reputations, PR began to be seen as a strategic asset. It evolved from mere media relations into a tool for reputation management, stakeholder engagement, and crisis communication.

The rise of digital media accelerated this shift. With the advent of social media and online platforms, PR moved beyond press releases and editorials. It embraced real-time engagement, storytelling, and content creation—making it indispensable in the digital age. Today, PR professionals work closely with marketing and brand teams to craft cohesive, multi-channel campaigns.

PR in India has truly come of age. It is now recognized as a core part of brand strategy. But the journey has not been easy—it has been shaped by the dedication and resilience of countless professionals who believed in its potential and pushed boundaries to establish its value.

This book is a reflection of that journey. Based on my own experiences across decades in the field, it covers the fundamentals of PR, strategic approaches, and real-world examples. It is meant to guide young professionals seeking a career in PR and offer perspective on where the industry is heading. Above all, it is a tribute to the passion and perseverance of those who have helped shape PR in India into the respected discipline it is today.

Dedication

This book is dedicated to those whose presence and influence have left a lasting mark on my life.

To my late father, Shri P. S. Viswanathan—a man whose dedication to his profession and steadfast principles continue to inspire me. His passion for banking and his quiet strength shaped my values and guided me through every phase of my journey.

To my late father-in-law, Shri P. N. Subramaniam—whose depth of knowledge and experience in the tyre industry offered not just professional insight but life lessons. Our many conversations remain with me as treasured memories filled with wisdom and encouragement.

To my wife and family—your unwavering support, quiet strength, and constant encouragement gave me the confidence to think differently, to take the road less travelled, and to pursue innovation. Your belief in me made all the difference.

Author's Profile:

Ganapathy Viswanathan is a distinguished communication consultant with over 30 years of transformative experience in the ever-evolving arenas of advertising and public relations. His professional journey has traversed some of the most iconic names in the industry—Ogilvy, Lintas, Mudra, and the Publicis Group—where he mastered the art of brand storytelling, strategic planning, and integrated communications.

With a rare blend of strategic acuity and creative vision, Ganapathy has spearheaded high-impact campaigns that have shaped brand narratives and earned acclaim on both national and international stages. His multidisciplinary expertise spans sectors and formats, empowering clients to deliver award-winning campaigns that drive results, spark conversations, and leave a lasting legacy.

A firm believer in nurturing talent and giving back to the industry, Ganapathy has played a pivotal role in mentoring and inspiring the next generation of communication professionals. As a visiting faculty member at Mumbai's premier institutions, he shares real-world insights and thought leadership that bridge the gap between academia and industry.

Beyond the boardroom, Ganapathy's passion for sports, particularly cricket and badminton, reflects his dynamic personality. A former badminton player himself, he brings a player's insight to his writing—crafting nuanced, engaging stories on both sports through his widely appreciated blog.

Ganapathy Viswanathan stands at the intersection of creativity, strategy, and mentoring—an enduring force in the world of communications and a passionate voice in the realm of sports.

Mastering The Message: Advance Praise

"PR is not really a science it is the magic of human relationship and communication, without which humanity will cease to exist. As the communication landscape continues to evolve, so must the practice of Public Relations. This book offers a practical and insightful approach to modern PR, making it essential reading for both seasoned professionals and aspiring communicators."

Piyush Pandey, Chief Advisor,
Ogilvy India.

Public Relations, has grown far beyond its traditional role of press relations to become a vital part of modern marketing communication. In this insightful book, Ganapathy Viswanathan draws on decades of experience in advertising, media, and PR to explore the evolving role of public relations today. With brands increasingly using PR to build trust and connect meaningfully with audiences, this book offers a clear, engaging, and comprehensive overview–ideal for newcomers and communication professionals alike. A valuable addition to the field of marketing communications.

Ambi Parameswaran
Advertising Veteran, Independent Brand Coach &
Best-Selling Author

I've known Ganapathy as a colleague and a friend. Over the years, he has consistently offered insight, clarity, and a unique perspective on the evolving world of public relations.

This book distils his observations, experiences, and reflections on the transformational phases of PR in India. It speaks with equal relevance to seasoned professionals and those just embarking on their journey.

A quick read. A compelling one. And above all, a must-read for anyone in communications.

Ajay Kakar
Head - Corporate Branding, Adani Group

"I've known Ganapathy for years and have always admired his passion for communications, his knack for storytelling, and his gift for writing. So, I was delighted to review Mastering the Message. It's a tour de force on all things PR—thoughtful, timely, and insightful. I especially appreciated how it bridges timeless PR principles with today's influencer-driven landscape. This book is a must-read from someone who truly lives and breathes the craft."

Prakash Sangam CEO,
redBus

"Mastering the Message: A Practical Approach to Modern PR" by Ganapathy is a must-read for professionals seeking a comprehensive and actionable guide to Public Relations and Corporate Communication. Part One explores the evolution of PR and its relevance as a dynamic, evergreen career. Part Two dives into sector-specific strategies across technology, BFSI, sports, politics, crisis management, and more—clearly distinguishing B2B and B2C approaches. A distilled career's worth of insights, this book is an invaluable resource for today's PR practitioners.

Abraham Alapatt,
President & Group Head – Marketing, Service Quality,
Value Added Services & Innovation
Thomas Cook India Limited.

Communication has evolved faster than its practitioners. The definitions of ATL, BTL and TTL are being constantly reimagined. Yet, while tools and media may have become unrecognisable, the fundamentals of messaging remain. It is perhaps more important now than ever before for PR professionals to be rooted in the basics of stakeholder relations and ethical communication. I trust that this compilation of his writings, insights, and experiences from an industry veteran will provide valuable guidance and inspiration for the communicators of tomorrow

Gokul Krishnamoorthy,
Independent Content Consultant &
Marketing Columnist

Contents

PART I

PR AND ITS BEGINNING IN INDIA

1.
The Evolution of PR in India

In the early 1970s, organizations had in-house publicity departments, which also handled public relations (PR) as an additional function. At the time, PR was in its very nascent stage in India, with limited print publications available for dissemination. PR primarily involved issuing press releases and conducting one-on-one interviews with journalists in a friendly and informal manner. Organizations like the Public Relations Society of India (PRSI) and institutions such as the Xavier Institute of Communications (XIC) took the initiative to create awareness about PR and educate professionals on its importance as a strategic communication tool.

As we entered the 1980s, PR began to take shape in a more structured and organized manner. One of the defining moments for PR in India was the World PR Congress, held in Mumbai in the early 1980s, where the father of modern Public Relations, Mr. Sam Black, addressed a large gathering of PR professionals and practitioners. Around the same time, Ogilvy & Mather became one of the first advertising agencies in India to establish a dedicated PR division—Ogilvy Public Relations—aiming to offer reputation management and corporate image-building services to its clients. Several prominent organizations, including the UB Group, VST Industries, the National Egg Coordination Committee (NECC), and the National Dairy Development Board (NDDB), began to recognize PR as a valuable marketing communication tool and integrated it into their business strategies.

The Growth of PR Post the Late 1980s and into the 1990s

1. **Liberalization and the Media Boom** – The early 1990s marked a turning point for PR in India with the liberalization of the Indian economy. The entry of multinational companies (MNCs) into the Indian market created a need for structured PR campaigns to manage brand reputation, crisis communications, and media relations. With the proliferation of new media channels, including satellite television and business magazines, PR professionals had more platforms to leverage.
2. **IPO Boom and Financial PR** – The economic reforms of the 1990s triggered an influx of Initial Public Offerings (IPOs), requiring companies to build investor confidence through well-crafted PR campaigns. Financial PR emerged as a specialized domain, with agencies helping companies communicate effectively with stakeholders, analysts, and the financial press.
3. **Rise of Global PR Networks in India** – The early 2000s saw international PR networks entering the Indian market, either through joint ventures or acquisitions.

Leading global PR firms like Edelman, Weber Shandwick, Burson-Marsteller (now BCW), and Fleishman Hillard set up operations in India, elevating the standards of PR practice and introducing data-driven strategies, crisis management expertise, and integrated communication solutions.

4. **The Digital Disruption** – The advent of digital technology and social media in the late 2000s and 2010s brought about a paradigm shift in PR. Traditional PR, which once relied heavily on media relations, expanded to include online reputation management, influencer partnerships, social media engagement, and content marketing. Platforms like Twitter, LinkedIn, Instagram, and YouTube enabled brands to engage directly with their audience, making PR more dynamic and in real-time.
5. **The PR Landscape Today** – In the present day, PR has evolved into a multi-faceted discipline encompassing corporate communications, public affairs, crisis management, thought leadership, and digital storytelling. With data analytics and AI-driven insights playing a crucial role, PR professionals must now navigate a complex media landscape while ensuring authenticity, credibility, and meaningful audience engagement.

From a relatively modest beginning in the 1970s to becoming a strategic function integral to corporate and brand management, PR in India has come a long way. As technology continues to reshape communication, the industry must embrace innovation, agility and ethics to stay relevant in the ever-evolving business environment.

2.

Best Practices in Public Relations

Public Relations (PR) is more than just media outreach—it's a strategic communication function that plays a vital role in shaping public perception, driving brand awareness, and building long-term credibility. In today's highly competitive and digitally connected environment, businesses—especially in the technology sector—rely heavily on PR to strengthen their brand identity, influence stakeholders, and engage audiences authentically.

To be successful, PR efforts must be consistent, proactive, and rooted in clear strategy. Below are the best practices that organizations should follow to make the most of their PR investments:

1. Setting Expectations from the Start

A successful client-agency relationship begins with setting clear, realistic expectations. Transparency about timelines, goals, and potential challenges helps foster trust and collaboration.

- **Define Deliverables**: Create a roadmap that outlines expected activities and outcomes, broken into monthly and quarterly goals.
- **Establish Timelines**: The first month is typically a warm-up phase, where the brand is introduced to journalists and analysts. Significant coverage may not materialize immediately unless there is a compelling or breaking news angle.
- **Maintain Open Communication**: Hold regular check-ins to review progress, troubleshoot obstacles, and refine strategies as needed.

2. Setting Realistic and Measurable KPIs

Key Performance Indicators (KPIs) provide a quantifiable way to measure the success of PR campaigns. However, they must reflect what is realistically achievable based on the brand's current market position.

Examples of effective KPIs include:

- Number of media placements in Tier 1 publications
- Share of voice compared to competitors
- Sentiment analysis of media coverage
- Website traffic from PR-driven content
- Growth in social media engagement linked to earned media

KPIs should be reviewed and refined quarterly to remain aligned with evolving business objectives.

3. Defining Key Messaging and PR Objectives

Every strong PR campaign is grounded in clear, focused messaging. Vague or inconsistent messages confuse both the media and your audience.

- **Craft sharp, concise key messages** for each quarter that align with the company's broader goals.
- **Tailor messages for each audience**—from investors to consumers—while ensuring consistency in tone and positioning.
- **Reinforce objectives** through all PR outputs: press releases, interviews, social media, and contributed content.

4. Developing a Robust Content Calendar

A content calendar brings structure to communication efforts, ensuring that key messages are shared in a timely and coordinated manner.

- Include **editorial opportunities**, seasonal themes, and industry events.
- Plan for various content formats such as blogs, white papers, videos, webinars, and infographics.
- Schedule **internal alignment meetings** to coordinate messaging across departments (marketing, sales, product).

This proactive approach minimizes missed opportunities and keeps messaging consistent across all channels.

5. Choosing and Training the Right Spokesperson

A well-prepared spokesperson is critical to delivering your message effectively, especially in high-stakes interviews or public appearances.

Select someone who is not only articulate and credible but also passionate about the brand.

Invest in **media training** to prepare for tough questions and help them stay on message.

Regularly **brief the spokesperson** with talking points, competitive intelligence, and relevant context before any public engagements.

6. Using Press Releases Strategically

While press releases are a traditional PR tool, overuse or misuse can reduce their effectiveness.

- Focus on **newsworthy content** such as product launches, funding announcements, partnerships, or research findings.
- Supplement with **creative pitch emails** that highlight the relevance of your story to the journalist's beat.
- Avoid sending out press releases for routine updates that don't add value to the media or audience.

7. Building Journalist Relationships Through Meetings

Relationships are the bedrock of successful PR. Take time to cultivate them through regular, meaningful interactions.

- Schedule **face-to-face or virtual meetings** with journalists to introduce the brand and understand their interests.

- Share **exclusive insights or trend analysis** to become a valuable resource, not just a source of press releases.
- Host **media roundtables or background sessions** in key cities to expand your reach.

These efforts deepen media trust and improve the chances of your story being covered in the future.

8. Hosting Press Conferences for Major News

Press conferences should be reserved for high-impact announcements.

- Choose a **compelling venue** and **coordinate timing** with your PR agency to avoid conflicts with other events.
- Ensure all messaging is aligned and anticipate questions.
- Offer **press kits** and **one-to-one interview slots** to maximize media interest.

Done well, press conferences can generate a significant media splash and reinforce your brand's authority.

9. Using Thought Leadership to Stay Visible

When there's no breaking news, maintain visibility through authored articles, blog posts, and interviews.

- Use your spokesperson's voice to address current industry challenges, innovations, or predictions.
- Contributed content positions your brand as a **credible authority** and enhances its long-term reputation.
- Collaborate with reputable publications to reach targeted audiences and boost SEO.

10. Preparing a Crisis Communication Plan

Crises are inevitable, but damage can be minimized with a well-thought-out plan.

- Develop a **response framework** that includes roles, responsibilities, and messaging templates.
- Conduct **crisis simulation drills** to test team readiness.
- Monitor media and social media sentiment continuously so you can act quickly if needed.

Transparency, speed, and empathy are crucial when managing a PR crisis.

11. Embracing Digital PR and Influencer Engagement

The lines between traditional and digital PR have blurred. Digital PR helps expand reach and drive engagement online.

- Collaborate with **relevant influencers** and thought leaders in your niche.
- Leverage **SEO-optimized content** to boost search visibility and backlink profiles.
- Utilize **social media** to amplify media coverage and foster two-way conversations with audiences.

Digital integration ensures your PR efforts are aligned with how today's audiences consume content.

12. Measuring, Analyzing, and Refining

Measurement should be ongoing—not an afterthought. Use both quantitative and qualitative metrics to evaluate performance.

- Tools like media monitoring, sentiment analysis, and engagement tracking offer deep insights.
- Use these findings to identify what's working, what's not, and where to double down or pivot.

PR is an iterative process. Continuous learning and adaptation are what ultimately drive long-term success. By adhering to these best practices, brands can create a strong PR foundation that enhances reputation, fosters trust, and supports business growth—no matter the size or industry.

3.

Setting Client Expectations: The Foundation of Successful Engagement

Most of us get excited when we win new business after a very competitive multi-pitch presentation. Yes, we need to win business so that we can grow and expand the organization. Also, winning businesses helps the consultancy get exposed to new verticals and offers challenges to the PR professionals working in any PR consultancy to work on and understand new brands, enhancing their knowledge and experience.

Having said that, before your engagement starts with the new client, it is most important to get the client's expectations right at the start so that the partnership continues in the long term.

Also, most clients in today's competitive world look for a long-term partnership for PR and hence it is important to choose the right partner to build your brand. Nobody wants to move away from a consultancy in a short time, as it's a massive task to get the new consultancy aligned to the client's goals and thinking, and one will lose time. So, what are the key aspects one looks at in setting the expectations which both the client and consultancy agree upon and follow religiously?

Here are some of the basic hygiene factors one should look at once your engagement starts with your client.

1. **Team Structure:** Get your team structure in place. With so much of attrition happening in the PR domain, clients would like to see beforehand the team that will service the business. Ensure that the load-bearing of the team is right so that it does not affect your client, as many clients are not comfortable with teams working on multiple accounts.
2. **Documentation & Processes:** Please set timelines on when the minutes and documents such as the work-in-progress will be shared with the client. The client should not chase and remind you about the same. Hence, agree on a date and follow it.
3. **Commercial Terms:** Finance is the most important thing. Agree on the figure and ensure that the consultancy shares the matching deliverables and the team structure with the client before you move to the next stage.
4. **Messaging Workshop:** Insist on having a detailed workshop to understand the client's business and agree on the annual objectives and the strategy planned. Messaging for each quarter should be finalized well in time before the quarter starts. Every quarter you need to revisit this and seek concurrence from the client if that is being delivered as per the agreed objectives and goals set.

5. **Spokesperson Availability:** Getting the spokesperson on time is always a challenge. Hence, work out a system with the client to ensure that the spokesperson is available on time. Avoid your client cancelling any meetings with journalist frequently, as in the long run, this can hamper your relationship with the media. When it comes to relationship meeting with media, please make it amply clear about the purpose of the meeting. Caution the client not to expect any outcome from those meetings.
6. **Quarterly Review:** This is mandatory, and you should tell your client to block the calendar every quarter to review the output and the work-in-progress. Quarterly review is a good diagnostic tool to do any course correction in case the desired objectives are not met. So, it is important that this cardinal meeting should never be postponed and should happen on time every quarter.
7. **Proactive & Not Reactive:** Clients love and are always looking for value addition in their communication strategy. So, if you are a consultancy that is proactive and able to execute the ideas recommended without flaw, you will have an added advantage. However, here again, you have to be practical, as the proof of the pudding will be achieving quality outcomes that were agreed upon.
8. **ROI & Measurement:** Ultimately, you need to agree on how you will evaluate the performance of the consultancy and the team. Hence, it is important to identify and agree on the measurement that the client and consultancy will follow to review the effectiveness and the final outcome of the various PR activities. There

is always a difference of opinion when it comes to PR measurement, so this has to be cleared at the beginning and followed for the entire period. If required, create a sample demo of the measurement matrix you plan to follow to bring in total clarity.

Managing expectations is not rocket science, but it all comes down to being very clear in what you communicate to your client. One must be very sure about what you can achieve and what you cannot, so there is no ambiguity in the end.

Remember, your client's expectations are not just delivering results but quality results. Therefore, never over-promise and then struggle to deliver, as it is always better to play cautious and not surprise or shock the client. This will certainly help you manage clients better instead of always being caught on the back foot.

To conclude, we all know over a period of time PR has become a powerful tool for many clients. Just like other marketing tools in the business of communication, one needs to know how to use it and what you want to achieve in the end based on the objectives set.

Consultancies in India today are following the West and are moving very rapidly towards using PR as a great strategic tool and the focus is to build brands and monitor them carefully, and not just perform media relations and execute the same. Clients are also looking at value and not simply volumes. So, the importance of strategic lead PR comes in place. The importance of strategically lead PR has been followed by most consultancies to give the right solutions to clients and with the advent of social media, agencies are getting more equipped to make that happen.

While India is catching up and has made a good progress, but need of more digital efforts and leveraging digital should be the top priority for both agencies and clients.

4.

Building Brand Trust Through Public Relations

If you are a client or a brand, what do you expect from PR? The answer is simple and short. TRUST. We all know trust is a very precious commodity, which is built over a period of time, involving thousands of hours spent on many interactions and reaching various touch points. While it is easy to say, "I want to be a trusted brand," one must also realise that a lot of hard work goes into attaining that trust status.

Today, when you ask anyone what the brand TATA stands for, the reply will come in a fraction of a second: TRUST. But to achieve the status of trust, the brand has done something right consistently. Here, Ratan Tata has played a significant role; his value system, transparency, and the ethics he has followed have stood him in good stead. The legacy continues, and the brand is trying its best to hold on to that trust factor across all verticals and businesses in which they operate. Trust is a major asset of brand TATA, and it will take all necessary measures to safeguard that asset. In today's social media driven world, they must be all the more alert and agile in monitoring their brand reputation.

When you run or own a company, the more honest you are, the more it will help the brand to strengthen its credibility and trust. Trust is built over a period of time, and it is important for you, as a brand, to educate your audience by engaging across platforms and addressing their needs and grievances to instil that element of trust. In today's digital world, the trust factor can erode very quickly; therefore, you need to be agile, respond quickly and carefully, and repose that faith with your audiences in any given situation.

The CEO of the company is crucial in staying engaged with stakeholders to build trust and credibility. By being honest and transparent, you further strengthen the equity of the brand. If the CEO happens to be a thought leader in the industry, it will further help in building the trust factor and enhancing the image of the company. This is where the corporate communication team must work and engage closely with the leadership team in presenting the face of the company from time to time through various touch points with strong, forceful messaging. Frequent interaction with the media, with the right message and news, helps the organisation build a strong relationship with both the media and stakeholders to earn trust.

So, what are some of the key drivers one must focus to manage the trust of your brand:

1. Be honest and transparent in what you're communicating.
2. Define your values and stand by them.
3. Never shy away from the media.
4. Brands do land up in crisis, but you need to act fast and contain it.

5. Stay in touch with media and interact with them regularly.
6. Continuously provide them with good news from the organisation.
7. Show authenticity in what you do.
8. Avoid empty promises and exaggerated claims.
9. Monitor the health of your brand through brand audits.
10. Share your point of view on relevant industry story from your leadership team.

5.

Why PR Continues to Grow—And Will Only Grow More

Let me start with some hard data that points clearly why the PR industry is on a growth path. In one of the published data sourced from PRCAI (Sprint report 2022-23), the Indian PR industry is valued at around US$260 million, which is around ₹2100 crore. The global PR market is significantly larger, amounting to US$20 billion and ₹1,60,000 crore, with US firms accounting for 50% of the market.

The Asia-Pacific market is around ₹13,600 crore (US$1.7 billion), accounting for 8.5% of the global PR market. India's share remains negligible, but the growth potential is immense considering developments in marketing and communication field, with more clients realising the importance of PR.

The statistics paint a healthy picture of this industry, and while there is a light at the end of the tunnel, it is still bright and will only keep glowing as more brands start to believe in PR as a powerful communication tool alongside their other marketing and promotional efforts. Over the last two decades or so, the industry has grown with a growth rate of 13% in the year 2022, and is no longer seen as merely pushing press releases. Today, press releases have become passé, and the focus has moved more towards strategic direction.

The number of press conferences has also declined, unless there is something big and exciting to announce. Even media relations and editor lunches are not happening at the same rate as in the past. Today, there are big challenges in the field of communication, and more thrust is being given to reputation management, crisis management, and influencer marketing.

Here are my views and observations on what could work for the PR industry to make it bigger in a consistent way and match global standards, though we are still a long way off. Globally, PR is still viewed and measured more in terms of quality coverage, without giving any importance to the volume of clippings.

Create Belief in PR

Yes, while marketers have started to focus on PR, especially post-Covid, but it is the self-belief in marketers that will drive the importance of PR and how it will add value to the entire gamut of the marketing plan. When annual marketing budgets are planned, PR should be included in the media mix right at the beginning and should be considered in the overall marketing strategy, so that there is a perfect orchestration of what is being communicated using the various communication tools. A proper and sizeable budget should be earmarked for PR, and the team should continuously evaluate and gauge the effectiveness.

Volume vs. Value

For a very long time now, Public Relations has been an endless chase for maximum coverage. But now, more and more clients have realised that it is the quality of coverage with the right messaging that matters. So, clients have become conscious and are making agencies accountable and ensuring that the key messaging is delivered once the story gets published.

Gone are the days when volume was seen as the key measurement; new and better methods of measurement are being worked out with agencies to get the right picture after the end of every PR campaign. The shift from volume to value has brought in a sea change in the way PR campaigns are being evaluated.

Social Media/Influential Marketing

With the proliferation of so many channels in the online space, the need for better thinking and being agile has become the need of the day. Today, you need to stay relevant, and with very little time available to grab the attention of your audience–who are always on the go–your content creation, be it short or long, should have a good narrative that will be sticky. This is where agencies need to focus to meet their client's deliverables and build their reputation.

Applying the Right Measurement Technique

Measurement in PR has always been a subject of debate, and till today there is no concrete solution between clients and agencies on what is the best practice for measurement. The most common measurement still prevalent is calculating the advertising value, which presents a very inflated picture, and one is not able to judge the true value of how PR as a campaign has worked.

While the industry is working to arrive at the best practice, the sooner this is done and agreed upon, the credibility gap will still exist on what PR is actually delivering. The industry should put an end to the measurement debates and work out a formula that is universally acceptable across clients' agencies so that more clients will be motivated to look at PR in a big way for promoting their brands.

Content will Drive Business

AI and ChatGPT have already brought in some disruption in the market. It is believed that ChatGPT is expected to change the way business will be approached both in marketing and PR. While AI and ML are great technology tools which are good enablers, we still need PR professionals to strategically think and be innovative in their ideas.

Remember, you still need great ideas to make your story narrative interesting and compelling, which technology will only help you in further crafting your innovative content for your digitally driven audiences. This is where talent management and training will be very crucial for both agencies and clients to nurture and build upon to have a robust team.

Going forward, the industry definitely has a good future to grow and establish a sound position in the communication industry. Healthy and relevant conversations should keep happening on PR, and the industry bodies together with the client and agencies should collaborate and share knowledge and promote the value of PR at various forums.

We would need some global seminars and PR meetings to be held on PR from time to time to know what are the best practices that are working globally. With the importance of research and social media growing and becoming more relevant, we would be able to witness more research-driven PR campaigns which will make many brands embrace PR and make them deploy PR regularly and not tactically.

6.

PR As a Marketing Constant in an Era of Transformation

PR had long struggled for both respectability and clarity of purpose, but the industry has clearly overcome that today, and every brand is very closely embracing PR as an important communication tool when they draw their overall marketing plan for their company and their respective brands. Clients must now be more open to trying and exploring new avenues in PR and will be looking at more innovative ways to explore Public Relations, especially in today's digital world.

The year 2024 saw more openness and greater embrace of brands with PR, and it looks like the future will also drive many clients to examine and explore PR closely in their annual marketing plans. I personally feel we may not see any major shifts in 2025, as some of the challenges in the area of talent and content creation will continue to trouble the industry. Agencies will have to strengthen their technology setups and operations with the right talent so that they can manage clients and meet their expectations.

So, what can agencies do, and how can clients collaborate better with their PR partners to get their best for their brands from a communication point of view? Let us examine how PR can bring in that value and differentiation for the brands, enabling them to leverage this communication tool.

1. I think you cannot build a strong reputation for your brand without PR. To achieve trust and credibility for your brand, there is no other communication tool quite like PR. Yes, it is a slow process and it takes time, but once your brand establishes credibility, it will stay for a very long time—unless something really goes wrong with the brand.
2. PR can help both reputed brands and start-up businesses build their reputation. Some kind of self-belief should be instilled in the stakeholders' minds to make them believe that PR works. This can only happen once you explore that channel with clear clarity of thought.
3. Adaptability is possible when you think of PR. A PR campaign can work in synergy with advertising or any other 360-degree communication. While your messaging should fall within the broad pillars of the advertising campaign, you have the freedom to deviate and take a different approach to reach your audiences, as long as the core messaging remains the same.
4. Your credibility quotient has more weight as PR is built through third-party endorsements. Consumers and your end audiences tend to believe messages delivered by journalists more than those in paid advertising campaigns planted in various media.

5. Brands, in any case, invest a lot when it comes to advertising and promotional campaigns. So, compared to that, PR investments are less–but you need to have a clear thought process as to what will be the role of PR and how you will leverage it with your main campaign. The perfect orchestration and clarity between the two will bring results.
6. Brand building is a continuous process. Running an advertising campaign in long bursts will always be a challenge, keeping in mind the exorbitant media costs and cash outflow. Hence, you will be only able to run in short bursts by taking breaks. But with PR, you can continue your efforts at a relatively lower cost, maintaining a media presence even while staying out of the spotlight.
7. In today's dynamic media landscape, especially after the advent of social media the need for online reputation has become very pivotal. You cannot ignore from your brand being trolled, and you need to be agile and alert to take the remedial action in case your brand gets some negative publicity. Hence, the need for PR comes into play for brands to embrace it.
8. Education and awareness about the role of PR should continue. The more we run seminars and panel discussions, this will help in reaching the desired audiences. It is these seminars and conferences, with appropriate themes, which will help encourage more brands to embrace PR and more professionals to join the PR industry.

PR is now the most spoken-about communication tool, as more and more brands are embracing with lot of confidence. Clients have witnessed results in building the credibility of their brands. As we move forward, the PR landscape in India is undergoing a fascinating metamorphosis, driven by a dynamic fusion of digital innovation and more emphasis towards influencer marketing.

While growth depends on several internal and external factors, but the intent shown by many clients—both brick-and-motor and the startups—is a good sign for the communication industry. Network companies should use their global expertise and knowledge to widen the canvass for PR being an important communication tool for brands to continuously engage with and build their brands.

PART II

THE ROLE OF PR ACROSS SECTORS

1.

The Growing Need for Sports PR

Over the past two decades, the Indian sports landscape has witnessed a significant transformation. Once dominated solely by cricket, the spotlight now shines on diverse disciplines such as kabaddi, football, badminton, athletics, and even indigenous sports. With this diversification comes the need for a more strategic, professional, and nuanced approach to Public Relations–an area that remains underdeveloped but full of potential.

Why Sports PR Needs a Strategic Push

Despite the growing popularity and commercial potential of various sports, PR agencies in India have only begun to scratch the surface of what's possible in the sports domain. A large portion of the current focus remains on cricket, while other sports and their stakeholders–athletes, franchises, leagues, and sponsors–are often underserved.

Sceptics may question the business viability of sports PR outside of cricket, but the reality is different. Today, with rising advertising costs and content saturation, brands are increasingly turning to sports as a medium to connect emotionally with audiences. Sports PR, when done right, can offer a more affordable, authentic, and engaging alternative to traditional advertising, while simultaneously helping athletes and franchises build strong, enduring public personas.

The Untapped Potential:

- **Individual athletes** need professional image management and crisis communication support.
- **Emerging sports and leagues** require consistent media outreach to gain recognition.
- **Brands** look for storytelling opportunities that align with sports values such as teamwork, determination, and resilience.

Key Focus Areas for Sports PR

1. Promoting Lesser-Known Sports Through Sports Bodies

One of the biggest opportunities lies in collaborating with sports bodies to spotlight underrepresented sports. This includes promoting regional events, profiling athletes from small towns, and generating media interest around lesser-followed competitions. Through strategic PR, emerging talent can attract the attention of selectors, sponsors, and fans—ultimately contributing to a more balanced sports ecosystem.

2. Brand Visibility and Strategic Positioning

Sports PR offers immense value to brands aiming to stand out. Instead of just sponsoring events, brands can integrate themselves into the fabric of a sport through storytelling. For instance, a table tennis equipment company can collaborate with local academies and use PR to amplify its grassroots initiatives, gaining credibility and loyalty in return.

This strategy is particularly effective in tier-2 and tier-3 cities, where audiences are eager for role models and local sports success stories. Well-positioned PR campaigns can inspire entire communities while delivering tangible brand impact.

3. Educate, Inspire, and Engage the Public

There is a pressing need to educate audiences about the evolving sports landscape—new rules, upcoming stars, global benchmarks, and sports science. PR professionals can lead this charge by:

- Publishing athlete interviews and behind-the-scenes features
- Creating content around training methodologies and mentorship
- Highlighting India's growing participation in global sporting events

Such storytelling not only nurtures interest but also builds a culture of aspiration among youth.

4. Building Media Relationships

A critical pillar of successful sports PR is collaboration with sports journalists and influencers. Agencies must understand the editorial requirements of each publication and deliver newsworthy, well-researched stories. A sustained relationship with the media ensures better coverage and can positively shape public sentiment.

Case Studies: How PR Has Built Sports Brands

IPL Franchises: A Blueprint for Sports Branding

The Indian Premier League (IPL) is a prime example of how PR, combined with strategic marketing, has revolutionized sports branding in India. Each IPL franchise–whether it's the Chennai Super Kings, Mumbai Indians, or Kolkata Knight Riders–has leveraged PR to establish unique identities, strengthen fan engagement, and enhance brand loyalty.

From behind-the-scenes videos, exclusive interviews, and CSR stories to timely press releases and crisis communication, PR has helped these franchises stay in the public eye year-round–not just during the tournament. Social media amplification, influencer partnerships, and regional language campaigns have further extended their reach and relevance across diverse demographics.

For instance:

- **Royal Challengers Bangalore (RCB)** used PR to align their brand with youth culture and bold personalities.
- **Chennai Super Kings (CSK)** successfully portrayed themselves as the 'people's team,' emphasizing consistency, loyalty, and regional pride.
- **Delhi Capitals** rebranded themselves through targeted PR and social storytelling, transforming public perception over just a few seasons.

ISL and Olympic Sports: Rising on the PR Ladder

The Indian Super League (ISL) has used PR to position football as a serious professional sport in India, even in regions where cricket once reigned supreme. Similarly, the Tokyo Olympics marked a turning point, with PR campaigns highlighting the journeys of medallists like Neeraj Chopra, Mirabai Chanu, and Lovlina Borgohain. These efforts played a major role in sparking national pride and driving attention to sports that previously received minimal coverage.

The Road Ahead: Building a Sustainable Sports PR Ecosystem

Sports PR in India is still at a nascent stage, especially when compared to countries with more mature sporting cultures. However, the momentum is undeniable. With continued investment and innovation, sports PR can become a catalyst for the next phase of Indian sports evolution.

What's Needed Going Forward:

- **Specialized Talent:** PR professionals with domain knowledge, passion for sports, and storytelling skills.
- **Grassroots Integration:** PR campaigns that begin at the local level to nurture talent and build credibility.
- **Measurable Impact:** Agencies must offer clear ROI through metrics like media reach, sentiment analysis, and audience engagement.
- **Brand-Athlete Synergy:** PR should act as a bridge between athletes and brands, enabling mutually beneficial partnerships rooted in authenticity.

Conclusion: A Powerful Tool for a Sporting Nation

As India continues its journey toward becoming a multi-sport nation, the role of sports PR will only grow in significance. Beyond just managing the image of established stars, the real opportunity lies in shaping narratives around emerging athletes, regional leagues, and visionary brands.

By combining strategic communication, authentic storytelling, and media collaboration, sports PR can transform not just individual careers or franchises, but also the broader sporting culture of the nation.

2.

How Tech Brands Built Their Identity Through PR

The early 1990s marked a pivotal moment in India's economic and technological landscape. Liberalization opened doors for global tech players, introducing Indians to a wave of innovations—from basic personal computers to mainframes and mini-computers. However, this transformation came with challenges. At the time, technology was still a complex and unfamiliar domain for the average Indian. Jargon was misunderstood, and many professionals relied on on-the-job learning or enrolled in computer training programs from private institutes to catch up.

Corporates began investing in computer literacy to modernize departments like accounting, which became early adopters of data processing through Electronic Data Processing (EDP) units. Yet, this digital shift was met with scepticism. Concerns about the accuracy of computers, resistance from trade unions, and fears of job loss made the transition difficult. Amid this uncertainty, tech brands such as Symantec, Hinditron, Dell, ICIM, and IBM were among the few recognized names. To stand out and build trust, these companies needed more than just product advertisements—they needed to shape public perception and educate the market.

Why Advertising Wasn't Enough

While advertising played a role in generating awareness, it lacked depth and credibility. Ads ran in business newspapers, magazines, and emerging tech journals, but their messages were often technical, unclear, or too sales-oriented to win consumer confidence. Moreover, given the pace of technological advancement, consumers needed ongoing education and reassurance—something that one-way advertising could not provide.

The Rise of Public Relations as a Strategic Tool

This is where public relations (PR) stepped in. In the early 1990s, PR in India was still evolving, and there were no dedicated tech beats in newsrooms. However, as technology began infiltrating daily life and global tech brands like Microsoft and Intel entered the market, the media started to pay attention. Journalists began covering stories on tech innovations, corporate IT adoption, and digital literacy. PR professionals played a crucial role in facilitating this transition by simplifying complex technology for a non-technical audience.

Unlike advertising, PR offered credibility and depth. It enabled companies to shape narratives, address fears, and educate stakeholders—from decision-makers in large enterprises to end-users concerned about job security or tech usability. Well-crafted press releases, thought leadership articles, interviews, and case studies allowed brands to engage meaningfully with their audience.

Global and Indian Success Stories in Tech PR

Globally, technology brands have long understood the strategic value of PR. Tech giants like Microsoft, Intel, SAP, Oracle, Cisco, and Amazon used PR extensively in their formative years to build credibility and visibility. Google, for instance, rarely invested in advertising in India during its early years, relying instead on PR to create buzz around its search innovations, Gmail, and later, Android.

In India, homegrown success stories like Infosys also benefited from PR-driven branding. Their focus on transparency, leadership visibility, and thought-driven narratives helped build a reputation as a trustworthy global software powerhouse. Similarly, startups like Flipkart, Ola, and Snapdeal used a mix of traditional PR and digital storytelling to build brand value, especially when advertising budgets were limited.

The Evolving Role of PR in the Digital Age

As the internet and social media became ubiquitous, the PR landscape underwent a dramatic shift. Traditional PR still matters—it remains a critical pillar for reputation management and media relations. However, digital platforms have expanded the scope, speed, and influence of brand communication.

Key Benefits of Digital PR in Tech Branding:

- **Real-Time Engagement:** Social media platforms like LinkedIn, Twitter (now X), and YouTube allow brands to engage with stakeholders instantly, enabling real-time reputation management and faster response to crises.

- **Content-Driven Influence:** Blogs, white papers, webinars, and podcasts offer brands the chance to dive deep into topics, positioning themselves as thought leaders and building long-term credibility.
- **SEO and Discoverability:** Digital PR contributes significantly to search engine optimization. Quality backlinks from media coverage and third-party mentions improve search rankings, driving organic traffic and brand discovery.
- **Data-Driven Storytelling:** Digital platforms offer rich analytics. Brands can measure engagement, track sentiment, and fine-tune messaging based on real-time feedback, making campaigns more effective.
- **Influencer Collaboration:** Collaborating with industry influencers and tech reviewers adds another layer of trust and reach. Influencer-driven product demos and reviews often carry more weight with tech-savvy audiences than paid ads.
- **Community Building:** Platforms like Reddit, GitHub, Discord, and even Telegram allow tech brands to build and nurture niche communities. Engaging with developers, users, and partners through forums fosters loyalty and advocacy.

PR in Action: A Hybrid Approach for the Future

Modern tech PR is no longer confined to traditional media engagement. It's about creating a multi-channel ecosystem where earned media, owned content, and shared narratives work together. This hybrid approach ensures that tech brands not only reach their target audiences but also build trust and relevance in an increasingly crowded marketplace.

Today's PR professionals are brand storytellers, data analysts, digital strategists, and reputation guardians rolled into one. They work closely with clients to understand technology roadmaps, anticipate media interest, and co-create campaigns that align with business goals.

Conclusion: PR as a Driver of Trust and Transformation

From the early days of scepticism to today's fast-paced digital environment, PR has been central to how technology brands build trust, credibility, and identity. It helped bridge the gap between innovation and understanding—making the unfamiliar familiar, the complex accessible, and the future exciting.

As technology continues to evolve—through AI, cloud, cyber security, and beyond—PR will remain a key pillar in guiding public perception, humanizing innovation, and empowering brands to lead with authenticity.

3.

Financial PR: Building Investor Trust During IPOs

With a surge of companies launching Initial Public Offerings (IPOs) in rapid succession, the financial market is abuzz. The influx of startups entering the IPO scene has created heightened activity, with financial partners and merchant bankers working to ensure strong subscriptions. Oversubscription not only reflects investor confidence but also helps create a favourable investment climate.

Today's investors—both institutional and retail—are more informed and analytical. They conduct thorough research before investing, whether in IPOs or secondary markets. In earlier IPO eras, companies heavily invested in corporate build-up campaigns, including press conferences where leadership shared growth narratives and future plans to engage the media and public.

Now, more than ever, storytelling plays a vital role. Companies must present a credible and compelling narrative to earn investor trust. This is where **financial public relations** becomes critical—helping brands shape narratives, position themselves effectively, and communicate with clarity and credibility.

The Strategic Role of Financial PR in IPOs

Regulatory oversight by bodies like SEBI and RBI ensures stringent scrutiny of IPO-bound companies. As a result, organizations are increasingly mindful of their messaging. Financial PR professionals help simplify complex financial data, presenting it clearly and consistently to media and stakeholders.

PR firms today integrate teams with deep knowledge of financial markets, regulatory frameworks, and investor behaviour. Their role is to decode financial statements and forecasts, avoiding any ambiguity that might erode investor trust.

The rise of social media and influencer-driven content has reshaped how financial PR is executed. Financial blogs, online forums, and commentary by finance influencers now play a pivotal role in shaping public opinion. However, all external communication is carefully monitored by regulators, ensuring that only verified and compliant information reaches investors.

Financial PR: A Bridge to Investor Trust

Financial PR is crucial in building trust with stakeholders—be it customers, partners, or investors. It helps reinforce the message that a company's business model is solid, its performance sustainable, and its future promising.

Effective financial PR is not built overnight. It requires a sustained, strategic effort that aligns public messaging with the company's financial goals and regulatory compliance. Social media campaigns, thought leadership content, and transparent communication from company leadership are all part of this broader effort.

In today's media landscape, companies are also using digital platforms—including the social handles of senior leadership—to amplify their messaging and engage audiences directly. Whether it's product innovation, hiring initiatives, or corporate milestones, social media helps drive conversations and increase visibility.

Industry Dynamics and the Power of Financial PR

Financial PR has become an essential source of trusted information for retail consumers, especially within the BFSI (Banking, Financial Services, and Insurance) sector. The growing number of IPOs and their strong market reception have increased consumer interest in financial products and services.

The IPO process should not be viewed merely as a fundraising event but as an opportunity to build long-term brand equity. Many IPOs today involve offers for sale by existing investors, which highlights the need for broader investor education. While retail investors often chase listing gains, understanding fundamentals like profitability, scalability, and governance is essential for sound decision-making.

Continuous PR outreach ensures that investors aren't swayed only by market sentiment or grey market speculation but are guided by facts, context, and credible analysis.

Digital PR: The Future of Financial Communication

The shift towards digital has been accelerated by global events like the pandemic, which drastically changed media consumption habits. What was once a balanced mix of traditional and online PR is now heavily skewed towards digital.

Digital financial PR allows companies to engage potential investors across multiple online touchpoints—blogs, news portals, social media, and more. By leveraging analytics and tracking conversational patterns, companies can tailor their messaging to align with investor concerns and trends.

As consumers grow increasingly self-reliant in sourcing financial information, digital PR becomes central to investor engagement strategies. In the BFSI sector especially, digitization is driving not just product delivery but also how companies communicate their value proposition to the market.

Conclusion

Financial PR is no longer just a support function—it is a **strategic necessity** for companies looking to build credibility, particularly when going public. In the current IPO climate, where investor scrutiny is high and information moves fast, well-executed financial PR ensures that companies tell their story authentically, transparently, and effectively. Whether through traditional media, digital platforms, or influencer networks, financial PR continues to shape perceptions, influence investor decisions, and build lasting brand value.

4.

PR In Political Campaigns: Challenges and Strategic Partnerships

The major national elections took place in 2024, and many political parties planned their PR campaigns with PR consultants to project a positive public image before voting. Public relations play a significant role in building credibility. The role of PR here is to help and play an immense role across the country, especially in the smaller towns, where it can help build some credibility—although the voters are quite aware and have their own perceptions about the various political party. It is a huge challenge to handle any political party, be it advertising or PR, as one has to deal with multiple leaders at various levels and hierarchies. Even PR agencies will always be cautious about signing a political party, as it demands 24x7 service, with adequate machinery on its toes and being always agile by monitoring and tracking news by the hour to get some valuable insights for the campaign and the messaging.

Political parties normally appoint a campaign committee who are given the sole responsibility to deal with agencies. They lay out certain rules, and broadly, they will try to stay within the boundaries of the election manifesto. Most big political parties have their own PR cells, who have fairly good contacts with the media. But when it comes to a national election—which is voluminous to handle—the role of a PR agency will really strengthen their position to professionally handle the communication strategy using the right tools for research and getting the correct messaging in the right media.

A political campaign is like any other FMCG campaign, as at the end of the day you are talking to consumer—who is the voter. However, while there will be an overall theme for the party at the national level, you still have to tweak you campaigns in each region based on the sentiments in each state and in their local language. In the last election, while there was social media, it was traditional media that still played a leading role. But during the recent elections, with the rapid penetration of the internet, the role of social media was more intense in terms of voter engagements. So, the entire media strategy here was much different from what we saw in the last elections. You would need a strong media cell that can devise a razor-sharp media strategy.

So here are my thoughts on what PR companies should know and follow if they are invited to pitch for a political party. And remember, normally this will be only for a short period, like a project, and you cannot expect them to be on an annual retainer, as one is not sure what will happen after the election results.

- Insist that you get a written brief with clearly defined objectives from the team with whom you are going to work with. Appoint a single point of contact to manage and disseminate all communications on behalf of the party.

- Insist that you decide on who will be the spokesperson for the party, and ensure that he or she is well-trained to talk to the media.
- From the agency side, you should have a complete team dedicated to handle the business, and all of them should have their ears and eyes to the ground to know what's happening around in the political environment.
- You will need a dedicated research team to continuously provide insights for the overall and tactical messaging from time to time.
- The language cell has to be well-equipped to get the right messaging in the regional towns. Smaller towns are big for political parties.
- Crisis can erupt at any time. So, ensure that you have a good crisis team, and you must frame a set of rules that you will follow to handle the crisis, which you need to get approved by the party spokesperson.
- Constantly be in touch with journalists and keep pumping them with useful and relevant information which will help the party.
- The political parties are also usually strong with certain media. This you need to understand right at the beginning and handle carefully without hurting the ego of the leader at the party.
- Stay connected with the party officials continuously throughout the day to know if they have some new insights to share. And at grassroot levels, they have

workers who will share titbits information from each state.

- How do we measure PR campaigns for political campaigns? This is one thing you should iron out at the beginning. Most of these parties will look at the volume of clippings to know if it is reaching everyone.

Handling a political account is far different from handling a government account. You need a different approach, as your communication strategy has to be very sharp and focused, and should touch the emotional chord of the voter–young and old. You also need to be clear about your commercial process and ensure that you talk it over right at the beginning your financial terms. The fear of not getting paid, which has been the fear of many agencies, has forced them to stay away from handling political campaigns. This is something the management has to think beforehand, before accepting the business. While the money could be huge, there is also an element of risk you need to foresee.

5.

Thought Leadership Through PR: Building A Lasting Voice

Thought leadership is a big buzzword in the business and corporate communication world, where every other leader wants to reach that position in quick time. As part of their PR brief, many clients have this habit of saying that our spokesperson should attain the thought leadership position at the earliest possible time once we start engaging with the media. While that is easier said than done, there is a lot of process and method involved in reaching the thought leadership status in any category or vertical that you are in.

To begin with, a lot of experience in the chosen field matters a lot. He or she should add value and be looked upon as a role model and subject matter expert. One must move beyond the conventional wisdom of old ideas and think boldly with new and disruptive ideas. They should be in the limelight and must constantly engage with media so that valuable insights flowing from their mind will attract a lot of followers. Writing regular pieces on their specialized subject will further boost the credibility and image of being recognized as a thought leader.

Remember, thought leaders are not born overnight but become leaders over a period of time, with vast knowledge and experience which they pass on to society at large through various platforms. You need to build transparency and credibility with your audience as a resource and as an expert on your chosen topic or industry. A thought leader is an individual or an organization that is excelling in the business it exists and has the expertise to talk about the community at large.

As a thought leader, one needs to set some examples as a leader that should inspire your followers, and they should keep following you through various social media platforms, looking for new ideas from you from time to time that can change their life. A long time ago, we had Mr. N.R Narayana Murthy of Infosys as a thought leader in the technology space. Similarly, in Advertising and Communication, we have Mr. Ambi Parmeswaran, a well-respected professional who has spent many years in the advertising and marketing field as a thought leader, sharing his views and ideas. He, even today, shares his point of view on various branding and advertising topics across various media channels.

In today's fast-changing world, thought leadership is expected to become increasingly important with the rise of digital and the internet, and with the increase in the number of customers who are well-informed. A well-planned thought leadership campaign can help in heightening brand awareness, boost traffic, and generate sales. It also helps in building the brand and strengthening its equity in the market.

What are some of the areas one must look at to build the stature of your leadership team as thought leaders?

1. Need to keep writing on a regular basis. A good authored article in a leading media outlet from time to time will build your credibility.
2. Participate in industry stories in your field of expertise with your point of view at regular intervals.
3. Create and build a personal blog of yours which should have fresh and interesting content that will excite the audience. Mr. Santosh Desai, a leading marketing guru, writes in The *Times of India* on regular basis, which draws a lot of attention and traffic. He has created a niche for himself, and today he is one of the most well-respected thought leaders in marketing and advertising.
4. You also need to give importance to your personal branding while you are in the thought leader position. That will heighten your awareness.
5. I will also suggest one-on-one leadership coaching for the thought leaders to gain that extra confidence and speaking skills.
6. Need to learn the art of storytelling, which will help in engaging better with your audience.
7. Always give a different point of view and ensure that you are factually correct in what you are saying.
8. Your messaging has to be consistent, simple and clear. The net take-out from your quote or message should be sticky and easily remembered by the audience.

As we are a growing nation, we need more experienced and mature leaders who are knowledgeable and are able to drive growth both for their company and the industry they are in. A thought leader with good thinking and innovative ideas will always bring in fresh perspective, which the government and various public bodies will look forward to and will also take the assistance of these leaders to frame regulatory policies.

6.

Crisis Preparedeness: Why Being Crisis-Ready Is Business-Smart

In today's dynamic and unpredictable business environment, crises can erupt at any moment, often without warning. Whether it's a financial scandal, a data breach, or a social media backlash, being unprepared can have serious repercussions on a company's reputation and operations. Therefore, it is essential to be crisis-ready rather than react with panic.

The Need for a Robust Crisis Plan

The cornerstone of effective crisis management is preparation. A well-structured crisis plan not only enables quick and efficient responses but also mitigates potential damage to the company's brand and business. To craft a reliable plan, businesses must identify key personnel, structures, and processes, ensuring that everyone involved knows their role when a crisis occurs.

A crisis action plan should include a simple checklist of responsibilities and actions to streamline the response. Regular rehearsals and simulations will help reduce confusion during actual crisis situations.

Forming a Crisis Management Team

An effective crisis team is the backbone of any crisis management strategy. This team is responsible for making key decisions and handling internal and external communications. Team members are chosen based on their skills and experience, and they must be prepared to act promptly when a crisis hits.

Key Roles in a Crisis Team:

- **Crisis Leader:** Directs overall strategy and decisions.
- **Spokesperson:** Communicates with stakeholders and the public.
- **Legal Counsel:** Advises on legal implications.
- **Media Liaison:** Handles media relations and briefings.
- **Information Gatherer:** Collects and verifies facts.
- **Technical Support:** Manages technical aspects related to the crisis.

Given the speed at which crises unfold, especially with the rise of social media, the crisis team must be available around the clock and able to assemble at a moment's notice.

Ten Cardinal Principles of Crisis Management

- **Stay Calm and Establish Facts:** Verify the accuracy of the information and determine responsibility. Respond only when fully informed.
- **Designate a Spokesperson:** Identify who will communicate on behalf of the company in advance.

- **Share Contact Information:** Make sure all key personnel are reachable, including legal counsel.
- **Agree on Messaging:** Define what to say and how to say it, targeting the appropriate audience.
- **Ensure Technology Readiness:** Make sure all communication systems are functioning properly.
- **Minimize Interference:** Avoid last-minute message changes, especially from senior management.
- **Media Training:** Equip all media-facing representatives with the necessary skills to handle inquiries.
- **Document All Interactions:** Keep records of calls, interviews, and statements for reference.
- **Prioritize Internal Communication:** Ensure the corporate communication team is the first to be informed.
- **Maintain a Journalist Watchlist:** Keep track of journalists who may have a critical stance towards the company.

The Role of Digital Monitoring

In the digital age, crises can escalate rapidly due to social media and online platforms. Investing in digital monitoring tools or partnering with agencies to track online mentions and breaking news can be invaluable. Early detection allows companies to respond promptly and mitigate the fallout.

Crisis Management: A Strategic Necessity

A crisis can either weaken or strengthen a company, depending on how it is handled. Being prepared is not just a defensive strategy—it is also a proactive approach to safeguarding the company's reputation and sustainability. Stay prepared, stay resilient.

7.

Celebrity PR: Evolution, Challenges, And Opportunities

How Has Celebrity PR Evolved?

Celebrity PR has seen a tremendous evolution over the past few decades. From the days when newspapers and radio were the primary mediums to today's digital era, where social media reigns supreme, the role of PR professionals in managing celebrities has changed significantly. Today, more than mere publicity, celebrity PR involves shaping and maintaining a personal brand, engaging with audiences, and navigating the ever-changing digital landscape. Let's delve into how celebrity PR has evolved, the challenges it presents, and the secrets to managing it.

Traditional Media to Digital Domination: Earlier, celebrity PR focused on managing public perception through traditional media like newspapers, magazines, television, and radio. PR professionals were tasked with crafting press releases, arranging interviews, and organizing public appearances. Today, the landscape has shifted dramatically. Social media platforms such as Instagram, Twitter (now X) and YouTube have taken center stage. Celebrities now have direct access to their audience, allowing them to communicate instantly without the need for a media filter. As a result, PR has evolved from being reactive to proactive, with digital strategies at the forefront.

The Rise of Personal Branding: In the past, celebrities were known primarily for their professional achievements. Today, they are seen as brands themselves. Whether it's a Bollywood actor, a cricket star, a fitness coach, or a celebrity chef, they are constantly working on building a distinct persona. This requires consistent messaging and storytelling, highlighting not just professional accomplishments but also personal stories, values, and lifestyle choices. The goal is to make the celebrity relatable and aspirational, allowing fans to connect on a deeper level.

Integrated and Strategic Approach: Modern celebrity PR is no longer limited to handling crises or managing events. It has become a comprehensive strategy that includes content creation, social media management, brand collaborations, and community engagement. PR professionals today need to be adept at creating multi-platform campaigns that align the celebrity's image with their goals, endorsements, and social causes.

Real-Time Engagement and Instant Communication: One of the most significant shifts in celebrity PR is the move towards real-time engagement. Social media allows celebrities to address their audience directly—whether it's to share good news, promote a project, or address a controversy. This immediacy requires PR teams to be vigilant, monitoring platforms constantly and being prepared to respond quickly. A delayed or poorly crafted response can damage a celebrity's reputation.

Data-Driven Decision Making: Today, PR strategies are increasingly data-driven. With tools to monitor engagement, sentiment, and online behaviour, PR professionals can analyse what works and what doesn't. Data helps in personalizing content, predicting fan reactions, and planning more effective campaigns.

Collaborative Branding: Collaboration has become a key element in celebrity PR. Celebrities frequently work with brands, influencers, and other public figures to expand their reach. These collaborations not only boost visibility but also reinforce the celebrity's brand identity. For instance, a fitness coach teaming up with a sportswear brand or a chef collaborating with a culinary product line helps create synergy and enhances personal branding.

Humanizing the Celebrity Persona: Modern audiences are drawn to authenticity. Fans appreciate when celebrities share their struggles, failures, and personal stories. Therefore, PR strategies increasingly focus on humanizing celebrities by presenting them as real people with relatable experiences. This approach helps build a loyal fan base and fosters trust.

Challenges in Managing Celebrity PR

Navigating the 24/7 News Cycle: In the digital age, news travels fast. A small incident can go viral within minutes, and managing the fallout can be daunting. PR professionals need to be prepared with crisis management plans that address potential controversies before they spiral out of control.

Balancing Privacy and Publicity: While fans crave access to celebrities' personal lives, maintaining boundaries is essential. PR teams must ensure that while celebrities remain relatable, their personal space is respected. Leaks or breaches of privacy can have severe repercussions.

Mitigating Social Media Backlash: One wrong tweet or post can ignite a firestorm. Celebrities need to be mindful of their online presence, and PR professionals often guide them on how to engage thoughtfully. In cases where backlash occurs, timely apologies or clarifications are crucial.

Maintaining Brand Consistency: With celebrities often juggling multiple endorsements, films, or projects, it's vital to maintain a consistent image. PR professionals work to ensure that brand alignments do not contradict the celebrity's core values.

Secrets to Successful Celebrity PR

Be Proactive, Not Reactive: Planning ahead is crucial. PR teams must anticipate potential controversies and have strategies in place. Building positive narratives proactively can also help cushion the impact of negative news.

Stay Authentic: Audiences today are quick to spot insincerity. Authenticity is key, whether it's addressing mistakes, sharing personal insights, or supporting causes. Celebrities who genuinely connect with their audience tend to enjoy sustained popularity.

Media Training and Preparedness: Training celebrities on how to handle interviews, public appearances, and social media interactions helps them navigate tricky situations with poise. PR teams often simulate challenging scenarios to prepare celebrities for tough questions.

Build Positive Associations: Incorporating social causes or community involvement into a celebrity's brand strategy helps build a positive image. Endorsing causes that resonate with their audience not only enhances credibility but also strengthens their personal brand.

Conclusion

Celebrity PR has come a long way from its traditional roots to becoming a dynamic and multifaceted discipline. As celebrities increasingly become brands in their own right, managing their public image requires strategic thinking, real-time engagement, and a deep understanding of digital landscapes. The challenges are manifold, but with the right approach, PR professionals can not only manage crises but also build lasting and meaningful connections between celebrities and their audiences.

8.

Understanding the Subtle Differences Between B2B and B2C PR

When discussing whether PR strategies differ between B2B and B2C brands, the answer is nuanced—both yes and no. At their core, the principles of public relations—building reputation, trust, and visibility—remain consistent across both. However, the way these principles are applied varies significantly due to differences in audiences, messaging, channels, and business objectives. Historically, B2B brands, especially those in the technology sector, were among the earliest and most avid users of PR.

These brands faced the unique challenge of demystifying complex products and technologies to a limited, highly specialized audience. With fewer communication channels available—mostly trade publications, specialized media, and industry events—B2B PR focused heavily on educating decision-makers and analysts, establishing thought leadership, and building credibility over extended sales cycles. On the other hand, B2C brands traditionally leaned more heavily on advertising than PR, given the need to appeal to a broad consumer base with emotionally compelling and attention-grabbing campaigns.

Unique Challenges Faced by B2B PR

The challenges faced by B2B PR practitioners are distinct. They need to simplify often highly technical or specialized offerings into clear, relatable messages that resonate with niche audiences such as industry professionals, procurement teams, or analysts. Unlike B2C, where the buying decision can be immediate and driven by emotion or trends, B2B decisions often involve longer sales cycles, multiple stakeholders, and complex evaluation processes. Therefore, B2B PR must support multiple touchpoints, including media relations with trade journals, analyst briefings, and the production of educational content such as whitepapers and case studies. The ultimate goal is to build trust and credibility over time, often through sustained thought leadership and consistent, authoritative communication.

Distinct Hurdles for B2C PR

Conversely, B2C PR operates in a much more crowded and fast-paced environment. The sheer volume of brands competing for consumer attention means that standing out is a major challenge. Messaging in B2C PR must be succinct, emotionally resonant, and memorable, often designed to quickly capture attention and inspire action. The channels involved range from lifestyle and entertainment media to influencers and social platforms where virality can be a game-changer but also a risk, as brand narratives can easily spiral beyond control. Additionally, crisis management and rapid response become critical given the high visibility and speed at which information spreads in consumer markets.

How PR Has Evolved for Both B2B and B2C

Over time, the PR approaches for both B2B and B2C have evolved and, interestingly, converged in several ways. Modern B2B PR is no longer just about dry, technical communication; it now incorporates storytelling, customer success narratives, and content marketing to humanize brands and make their value propositions more relatable. B2B brands leverage social media, podcasts, webinars, and video content to engage their audiences more dynamically. Similarly, B2C PR has grown beyond simple brand awareness to emphasize authenticity, social purpose, and experience-driven engagement, often through collaborations with influencers and leveraging user-generated content. Both sectors now view PR as a strategic tool to build community, enhance brand reputation, launch new products, and support broader marketing and business goals.

The Transformative Role of Social Media

The rise of social media has profoundly transformed the PR landscape for both B2B and B2C brands. For B2C brands, platforms like Instagram, Facebook, and YouTube have become vital for real-time engagement, influencer partnerships, and viral campaigns that can rapidly amplify brand messages or, conversely, expose vulnerabilities. B2B brands have also embraced social media, particularly LinkedIn, Twitter (now X), and YouTube, as essential channels for thought leadership, industry conversations, and lead nurturing. Social media's direct-to-audience communication model enables brands to bypass traditional gatekeepers like journalists and analysts, accelerating message delivery and feedback loops. However, it also requires greater agility and vigilance, as narratives can evolve quickly, demanding swift and strategic responses.

Strategic Approaches to PR for B2B vs. B2C

Strategically, approaching PR for B2B versus B2C requires tailored frameworks. B2B PR must focus on targeted audience segmentation, developing content that educates and informs, and leveraging industry-specific media channels. It emphasizes long-term relationship-building with key stakeholders and often integrates PR with sales and marketing efforts to support lead generation and customer retention. B2C PR, meanwhile, prioritizes broad-reaching campaigns that connect emotionally with consumers, utilizing mass media, influencers, and experiential marketing to build awareness and loyalty. Messaging is crafted to be relatable, timely, and often tied to lifestyle or cultural trends. The tactics may include product launches, brand activations, and storytelling that highlights brand values and consumer benefits.

Final Summary: Shared Foundations, Different Execution

In conclusion, while B2B and B2C PR share foundational goals, their execution diverges to address different audience expectations, communication challenges, and business objectives. The digital era and the proliferation of social media have blurred traditional boundaries, enabling both sectors to adopt more integrated, authentic, and responsive PR approaches. Effective PR today requires a strategic blend of storytelling, targeted media engagement, and agile communication that is aligned with evolving consumer and business landscapes. Whether B2B or B2C, PR is no longer a peripheral activity but a critical driver of brand reputation, engagement, and ultimately business success.

PART III

MEDIA RELATIONS

1.

Crafting The Perfect Pitch: How to Capture Media Attention

Introduction

A well-crafted, perfect pitch can truly captivate a journalist. In today's fast-paced media environment, simply creating a press release and disseminating it for minor coverage is no longer effective. Despite the notion that press releases are passé, many clients still insist on mass distribution, often leading to the press release landing in a journalist's spam box. Journalists today are more discerning and look for engaging, original stories that provide value to their readers.

Journalists across all platforms–print, digital, or broadcast–are incredibly savvy and have their ears to the ground. They constantly seek proactive briefings or story angles that stand out. Hence, a well-thought-out pitch with clear and compelling messaging can make a lasting impact, helping a brand build credibility.

The Art of Pitching: Why It Matters

An engaging pitch grabs attention instantly. A poorly constructed, vague, or uninspired pitch will never see the light of day. Crafting a pitch note is an art—it takes time, experience, and a deep understanding of both the brand and the journalist. Through brainstorming and client input, you can arrive at a killer strategy or news peg that genuinely excites a journalist to pursue the story.

Understanding the Journalist's Perspective

To craft the perfect pitch, it is crucial to understand the journalist's perspective. Analyse their past work, gauge their preferred style, and consider the types of stories they are likely to cover. Additionally, always evaluate whether your pitch is genuinely newsworthy. Using social media as an additional outreach tool can also facilitate faster responses and increase the chances of your story being picked up.

Key Drivers for a Great Pitch

- **Define Your Objective and Message:** Clearly outline your goal, target audience, and key message.
- **Know Your Industry:** Conduct thorough research to ensure that your insights and data are accurate.
- **Focus on Insights:** Strong insights add value and intrigue, making the pitch more compelling.
- **Be Concise:** Keep your pitch tight and to the point—something akin to an elevator pitch.

- **Incorporate Storytelling:** Human stories and relatable content make the pitch more engaging.
- **Add Value:** Support your pitch with credible data or anecdotes to strengthen its impact.
- **Brainstorm and Collaborate:** Engage your team to develop fresh, relevant ideas.
- **Be Innovative:** Think creatively to present your pitch in a unique and memorable way.
- **Personalization:** Customize your pitch for each journalist to demonstrate respect and understanding of their work.
- **Build Relationships:** Strong professional relationships with journalists can greatly enhance your pitch's success.

Formats and Techniques

To make your pitch truly compelling, experiment with various formats such as email pitches, video clips, or even audio snippets. However, nothing quite matches the impact of a face-to-face meeting where you can present your idea directly and address questions in real time. This personal touch can significantly enhance your pitch's effectiveness.

Final Thoughts

A compelling pitch is not just about conveying information; it's about telling a story, sparking curiosity, and demonstrating relevance. By meticulously planning and crafting your pitch, keeping it insightful and concise, and respecting the journalist's perspective, you greatly increase your chances of media success.

2.

The New Media Landscape: Does PR Have the Right Playbook?

PR is no longer just about relationships; it's about relevance. As the media landscape continues to shift, PR professionals must evolve from gatekeepers to collaborators, from storytellers to co-creators.

Based on my recollections of the late 80s, media relations were the driving force behind the PR industry. Many PR professionals would take it upon themselves to deliver the press release directly, engaging with either the editor or the bureau chief to ensure the news made it to publication.

In most instances, particularly when it pertained to financial results, the news was almost always published. The decision to publish hinged on the significance of the news.

The late 80s marked a significant era when IPOs made a grand entrance into the Indian capital market, capturing the attention of major financial news outlets and business publications alike. Since there were fewer media newspapers, the news would be carried in the next few days if not immediately.

The PR business purely thrived on good media relations, with minimal reliance on interview-based coverage. The limited media presence, primarily focused on print, allowed the PR team to effectively manage media rounds and maintain consistent communication with journalists.

Press conferences were well-attended, often drawing a full house of media representatives from various publications. Some even arrived uninvited, eager to partake in the generous spread of food and drinks.

With the swift evolution of technology, news is now disseminated via X (formerly Twitter) or through video conferences on platforms such as Zoom, where media representatives are invited to join online.

To attract media attention to the conference, you'll need to leverage your influence effectively. The media present today are exceptionally astute, arriving well-prepared and equipped with thorough research to pose insightful questions that will yield compelling stories for the following day.

Media relations are here to stay, but it's essential to enhance the value offered to the media community to foster a robust connection. I'm uncertain whether PR firms are systematically and scientifically harnessing this opportunity, especially as the media landscape continues to expand and evolve.

Earlier, we had a dedicated individual responsible for media relations, whose sole focus was to develop a comprehensive database of journalists, starting from editors and beyond.

However, with the rise of digital media and the swift expansion of the internet, the landscape of media relations has transformed significantly.

Today, it's essential to cultivate strong relationships with influencers, who wield significant power in the current social media landscape.

How well-versed are our media relations experts in the realm of social media today? This is a question to ponder.

The time has arrived for you to embrace multi-tasking and expand your knowledge of media relations. Relying solely on your media relations manager is no longer an option, especially in a large PR firm where they must serve the entire organisation.

The media landscape is undergoing a significant transformation, where personalisation and relationship building extend beyond traditional editors. Enter a new generation of experts: influencers and micro-influencers, who are now playing a pivotal role in shaping this dynamic environment.

In today's fast-paced environment, PR teams must remain agile and vigilant, ready to respond swiftly to media enquiries.

This proactive approach is essential for extinguishing potential fires and effectively managing any communication crises that may arise. In today's landscape, content is the driving force behind media and brands.

It's no longer just about pitching stories to editors and publications; co-creating content with them and influencers has become essential for amplifying your brand's presence across multiple media channels.

Media relations certainly haven't been completely sidelined. Your approach to engaging and working with media has transcended into a new realm. Media teams nationwide are under pressure to produce content swiftly, driven by the fast-paced evolution of the internet and social media.

They constantly race against the clock to craft compelling stories that influence perceptions of various brands with the perfect narrative. It's all about collaborating with media and infusing them with innovative ideas and pertinent content to create captivating stories that resonate.

PR professionals must stay ahead of the curve and explore innovative ways to collaborate with the media. Over the past decade, the industry has undergone significant transformation, and this evolution is set to accelerate, particularly with the rise of AI and data analytics.

The growing emphasis on authenticity and transparency is crucial for establishing trust in clients' brands. As a powerful marketing tool, PR holds tremendous potential to enhance the credibility of these brands.

To succeed and adapt in the ever-evolving media landscape, PR professionals must cultivate robust relationships with influencers and the media, while also creating captivating content and implementing effective PR strategies.

In today's landscape, media relations hinge on a deep collaboration with publications rather than merely fostering friendly connections.

As we navigate an increasingly competitive and evolving media environment, the concept of collaboration is poised to take precedence over traditional relations.

3.

Journalist Vs. Influencer: Understanding Credibility and Accountability

In the digital age, the lines between journalists and influencers can appear blurred, as both occupy online platforms and engage large audiences. However, their roles, responsibilities, and impacts differ significantly. While both contribute to the evolving media ecosystem, it is crucial to understand their distinct purposes and standards. This awareness is vital for navigating the media landscape with critical insight and digital literacy.

1. Credibility and Trust

Journalists strive for factual accuracy and public trust. Their credibility stems from professional training, adherence to ethical standards, and accountability to established editorial processes. They are expected to verify information, remain objective, and prioritize public interest over personal gain.

Influencers, on the other hand, build trust through personal branding, relatability, and consistent visual or stylistic presentation. Their credibility is often based on lifestyle expertise, personal experience, and audience engagement, rather than objective reporting or journalistic investigation.

2. Accountability

Journalists are accountable to their news organizations, editorial policies, professional codes of conduct, and, in many cases, regulatory bodies. They operate under public scrutiny and may face serious consequences—legal, professional, or reputational—for spreading misinformation or violating ethical norms.

Influencers typically operate independently or in partnership with brands, with accountability largely limited to their audience and sponsors. Mistakes or misinformation may lead to backlash or loss of followers, but there is usually no formal body to regulate or discipline their content beyond the platform's policies or public opinion.

3. Purpose of Content

The primary goal of journalism is to inform, investigate, and analyse issues that affect the public. Journalists aim to provide accurate, well-researched, and balanced reporting to empower citizens and uphold democratic values.

Influencers, by contrast, usually focus on entertaining, inspiring, or promoting products and trends. Their content is designed to drive engagement and personal connection, often emphasizing lifestyle, aesthetics, or brand alignment rather than in-depth public service reporting.

4. Impact on Public Perception

Journalists play a critical role in shaping public discourse through fact-based storytelling. Their investigations and reports can spark debate, influence public opinion, and lead to policy changes. Journalism is often a catalyst for civic engagement and social accountability.

Influencers shape public perception in different ways—mainly through setting trends, guiding consumer behaviour, and cultivating aspirational lifestyles. While they may influence cultural norms or occasionally highlight social issues, their content generally does not carry the same societal weight or investigative depth as journalism.

A Converging Landscape, But Distinct Roles

It's important to acknowledge that media boundaries are evolving. Many journalists now use digital platforms like YouTube, Instagram, and podcasts to reach broader audiences. Likewise, some influencers occasionally comment on current events or advocate for causes. However, this overlap does not erase the core differences in their goals, standards, and systems of accountability.

Journalists operate within frameworks that demand accuracy, ethical rigor, and service to the public good. Influencers function in an entrepreneurial ecosystem driven by metrics, branding, and platform algorithms.

Conclusion

While both journalists and influencers have influential roles in today's media environment, their **responsibilities, credibility,**

and societal impact differ significantly. Journalism remains a cornerstone of informed democracy—rooted in truth, ethics, and accountability. Influencers, though powerful cultural figures, primarily serve functions related to entertainment, marketing, and lifestyle.

Recognizing these distinctions is essential for digital literacy. It empowers audiences to assess content critically, understanding when they are being **informed**, and when they are being **entertained** or **marketed to**.

4.

Media Training Matters: Mastering The Art of Strategic Communication

In today's fast-paced media environment, where information flows continuously and public perceptions can be shaped instantly, effective communication has never been more crucial. For organizations, a skilled spokesperson can be the difference between a successful media interaction and a public relations disaster. This is where media training becomes indispensable.

Media training equips spokespersons with the necessary skills to confidently and effectively interact with the media. Even the most eloquent speakers can falter when faced with probing questions from journalists or the intense pressure of a live interview. The ability to handle such situations with composure and clarity is an art that needs honing.

What Goes into Media Training?

Media training is a structured process that prepares individuals to face the media with poise and precision. Here's what it typically involves:

- **Message Development:** The core of media training lies in crafting clear, concise, and compelling messages. Spokespersons are trained to distil complex information into easily digestible sound bites that resonate with audiences. This skill is crucial when speaking to diverse audiences who may have varying levels of familiarity with the subject matter.
- **Interview Techniques:** Training often includes practical strategies for managing interviews, including how to respond to tricky or unexpected questions without losing track of the core message. Techniques like bridging, flagging, and pivoting are taught to maintain control of the conversation. Additionally, understanding the nuances of different media formats—live TV, print interviews, or digital platforms—can significantly influence how one approaches each interaction.
- **Body Language and Demeanour:** Non-verbal cues can significantly impact how a message is perceived. Media training focuses on maintaining eye contact, adopting an open posture, and using hand gestures effectively. Maintaining calm and confident body language helps build credibility and rapport with the audience. Practicing these non-verbal aspects repeatedly can help the spokesperson appear more relatable and trustworthy.
- **Crisis Communication:** During a crisis, media interactions can be daunting. Media training prepares spokespersons to communicate transparently and calmly, preventing the escalation of negative publicity. It includes formulating responses that acknowledge issues

without admitting fault prematurely. Training also focuses on developing a crisis communication plan that outlines how to handle potential backlash and maintain public confidence.

- **Practice Sessions:** One of the most crucial elements of media training is practice. Mock interviews conducted under realistic conditions help spokespersons apply their learning, building familiarity and reducing anxiety when facing real scenarios. Role-playing with tough, uncomfortable questions prepares spokespersons to think on their feet.

The Benefits of Media Training

- **Enhanced Confidence:** Facing the media can be daunting, even for experienced speakers. Media training helps build self-assurance by familiarizing spokespersons with the dynamics of interviews and media interactions. Confidence translates to clarity and coherence in messaging. Moreover, having pre-prepared key messages allows speakers to stay focused even when faced with challenging questions.
- **Message Control:** Journalists often ask pointed or unexpected questions. Media training equips spokespersons with techniques to steer the conversation back to key messages. This helps ensure that the organization's narrative remains clear and consistent. By mastering the art of subtly guiding interviews, spokespersons can minimize the risk of being misquoted or taken out of context.

- **Crisis Management:** In situations of crisis or controversy, a well-prepared spokesperson can mitigate damage. Media training focuses on formulating responses that are honest yet tactful, helping maintain the organization's reputation. It also trains spokespersons to handle hostile questioning without appearing defensive or evasive.
- **Positive Brand Image:** A skilled spokesperson enhances the public's perception of the organization. They project professionalism and reliability, fostering trust among stakeholders. A well-prepared spokesperson can turn challenging situations into opportunities to reinforce the organization's values.
- **Reduced Miscommunication:** Poorly phrased statements can lead to misunderstandings or negative coverage. Training helps avoid ambiguous language and ensures that the intended message is conveyed accurately. By practicing concise and precise communication, spokespersons reduce the chances of being misinterpreted.

The Art of Handling the Media

While some individuals may naturally be good speakers, addressing the media requires a distinct skill set. Handling media interactions is not just about speaking well; it involves:

- **Managing Nerves:** Media interactions can be high-pressure situations, especially when broadcast live. Training helps speakers maintain composure and think on their feet. Staying calm is critical, as visible signs of stress can undermine the speaker's credibility.

- **Handling Tough Questions:** Journalists may probe for controversial or sensitive information. Media training teaches how to address these without appearing evasive. Techniques like acknowledging the question while redirecting to a key message can maintain the flow without sounding defensive.
- **Balancing Honesty with Diplomacy:** Being transparent while protecting the organization's interests is a fine line, and training helps find this balance. Spokespersons learn to express empathy and understanding without making commitments that could backfire later.

PR Agencies Must Prioritize Media Training

Public Relations agencies should make media training an integral part of their strategy. It's not enough to craft press releases or manage social media; the human element of communication is paramount. Media-trained spokespersons represent the organization with authority and credibility, leaving a positive impression even in challenging situations. Proactive media training also prepares organizations for crisis communication before issues escalate.

Conclusion

Media training is more than just a skill enhancement; it's an investment in an organization's reputation and communication strategy. Whether dealing with routine announcements or navigating a crisis, a media-trained spokesperson can make a significant difference. In an age where news spreads like wildfire, being prepared to face the media with confidence and clarity is no longer optional–it's essential.

PR agencies, in particular, should advocate for media training as a critical component of their client strategy. It empowers spokespersons to represent the organization effectively and helps maintain a positive brand image. Mastering the art of media communication is an invaluable asset that every organization should prioritize. In a world where perception can influence reality, media training ensures that your message remains strong, clear, and positively impactful.

PART IV

MANAGING TALENT IN PR

1.

Talent Management in the PR Industry

The public relations (PR) industry has undergone a seismic transformation over the last decade. What was once seen as a support function in corporate communication has now evolved into a strategic pillar essential to brand management, reputation building, and crisis mitigation. Today, there is barely an organization—large or small, private or public—that does not engage with PR in some form. In fact, most companies now have both internal corporate communications teams and external PR agencies working in tandem to manage their messaging across increasingly complex media ecosystems.

This transformation has brought with it tremendous opportunities, but also a new set of challenges—particularly in talent management. As the demand for strategic communication continues to grow in a digitally driven and reputation-sensitive world, so too does the demand for skilled PR professionals. However, the industry is currently facing a significant talent crunch, struggling to attract, train, and retain the workforce it needs to keep pace with its growth trajectory.

While there is no shortage of fresh graduates eager to join the PR industry, a critical gap remains in their job readiness. Many newcomers are entering the profession without adequate exposure to the practical, fast-paced, and high-pressure nature of PR work. Academic training often fails to align with industry expectations, and as a result, agencies are spending significant time and resources on training new recruits–time that could otherwise be spent on client strategy and execution.

The digital transformation, catalysed by the global pandemic, has only intensified these demands. Online reputation management, social media listening, influencer engagement, and crisis response now require real-time action and specialized skill sets. PR professionals are expected to be not just media experts, but also content strategists, data analysts, storytellers, and digital natives. This multifaceted expectation has created a scenario where the industry needs highly adaptable professionals who can work across platforms and disciplines–something the current talent pipeline is struggling to provide.

Further complicating matters is the evolving role of brand managers. Unlike in the past, today's brand custodians are actively investing in dedicated PR campaigns, viewing them as standalone strategies rather than mere extensions of advertising or marketing. This trend has led to increased demand for PR specialists who can offer high-level strategic counsel and execute sophisticated campaigns with measurable outcomes. As brand managers begin to understand and appreciate the impact of well-executed PR, they are raising the bar in terms of what they expect from their agencies–further stretching the limited pool of experienced professionals in the field.

However, while the external demand continues to grow, the internal culture of the PR industry has not evolved at the same pace. High levels of burnout, lack of structured career progression, and inadequate support systems have resulted in high attrition rates, especially among mid-level professionals. Many young entrants, despite initial enthusiasm, exit the profession prematurely due to the intense workload and lack of long-term visibility. This talent drain is particularly concerning, as it impacts the continuity and depth of experience within agencies and organizations.

To address these issues, the PR industry must first look inward. Ironically, despite being experts in managing reputation and building brands for clients, PR firms have historically done little to promote themselves as attractive career destinations. The industry must start practicing what it preaches—by developing strong employer branding strategies that highlight the dynamic, impactful, and rewarding nature of PR work. Just as organizations invest in campaigns to attract consumers, PR agencies need to launch targeted efforts to attract and retain top talent.

One of the most immediate areas of focus should be the academic-practical gap. Educational institutions and PR agencies must collaborate to design curricula that reflect real-world industry needs. This includes integrating live projects, industry mentorships, guest lectures from professionals, and internships that go beyond observation to hands-on experience. A more immersive and aligned educational journey can help ensure that graduates enter the workforce with realistic expectations and a stronger skill foundation.

Additionally, the industry needs to invest in mentorship, peer learning, and continuous upskilling. Creating structured onboarding programs, clearly defined career pathways, and opportunities for vertical and lateral growth can go a long way in retaining talent. Establishing a culture that values learning, creativity, and mental well-being is not just good for morale—it's a competitive necessity in a knowledge-driven field like PR.

Furthermore, PR associations and industry bodies should play a more proactive role in talent development. This includes launching awareness campaigns to attract young talent, organizing networking events, setting up knowledge-sharing platforms, and conducting certification programs. Such initiatives can demystify the profession, foster community, and build a sense of belonging among professionals at different stages of their careers.

Finally, agencies need to take the lead in changing perceptions about the profession. By telling their own stories—sharing behind-the-scenes wins, career journeys of their staff, and the impact of their work—PR firms can present a more accurate and inspiring picture of the industry. Social media platforms, alumni engagements, and speaking opportunities at student forums can all be leveraged to create a steady pipeline of informed and enthusiastic talent.

In conclusion, managing talent in the PR industry is a multidimensional challenge that requires systemic change. From rethinking how the industry attracts new professionals to ensuring that existing ones see a clear and fulfilling future, the responsibility lies with both agencies and educational institutions. As PR continues to grow in importance and influence, its ability to solve its internal talent crisis will be just as crucial as the reputations it builds for its clients. Only by investing in its people can the industry secure the vibrant, innovative, and resilient workforce it needs for the future.

2.

Building A PR Career: The Skills and Mindsets That Matter

Public Relations (PR) is a dynamic field that blends strategy, communication, creativity, and relationship management. At its core, PR is about building and maintaining a positive image and fostering meaningful connections between an organization and its stakeholders. Whether you're just starting out or looking to sharpen your skills, here are the key competencies and mindsets you need to develop to build a strong career in PR.

1. Master the Fundamentals of Communication

The fundamentals of PR will never change, no matter how much the industry evolves with new technologies or platforms. Every communication you craft should be **transparent, credible, and clear**. Clear communication eliminates confusion, builds trust, and enhances the reputation of your client or brand.

Clarity is the cornerstone of effective messaging. When you communicate clearly, your audience understands not just the message, but also the intent behind it. Developing the ability to strike the perfect balance between **strategy and execution** ensures that your messaging is consistent and aligned with campaign goals.

2. Build a Habit of Lifelong Learning

One of the most important habits for a PR professional is the constant pursuit of knowledge. This field requires you to stay up to date with industry trends, news developments, and shifts in consumer behaviour.

Make it a practice to read daily – newspapers, blogs, magazines, industry journals, and books. Build your own "knowledge library" by saving articles, white papers, and reports that could inform future campaign planning or strategy. Think of it as creating your personal Wikipedia on your laptop. Curating and referencing this content regularly will give you an edge when brainstorming ideas or handling complex PR challenges.

Reading not only boosts your knowledge but also strengthens your **writing and analytical thinking** – two of the most vital tools in PR.

3. Develop Excellent Writing and Presentation Skills

Writing is a non-negotiable skill in PR. Whether it's crafting press releases, blog posts, speeches, or social media content, you must know how to convey messages succinctly and persuasively.

Equally important is your ability to present ideas confidently. PR professionals frequently pitch campaigns to clients, make presentations to internal teams, and speak with the media. Developing **public speaking** and presentation skills will enhance your credibility and influence.

These abilities improve over time with practice and feedback, but showing a genuine **passion to learn and improve** will accelerate your progress.

4. Practice Active Listening and Observation

True communication goes beyond speaking and writing – it starts with **listening**. Whether you're receiving a client brief or conducting an interview, active listening helps you understand the core issue, identify nuances, and uncover insights.

Observation is equally powerful. Being alert to body language, tone, and context can help you better interpret situations and respond thoughtfully. Together, these skills enable you to ask the right questions – a must when working under tight timelines with journalists or during strategic campaign planning.

5. Hone Attention to Detail

In PR, the small things matter. A missed typo in a press release, a misquoted statistic, or a wrong date can damage your credibility. Clients and journalists expect you to be meticulous and accurate.

Before sending any document – whether it's a press note or an email – make sure it's **error-free and polished**. Attention to detail builds trust, and over time, you'll be recognized for the quality and professionalism of your work.

6. Think Creatively and Innovatively

Creativity is at the heart of standout PR campaigns. Journalists and clients are always looking for fresh, **innovative ideas** that cut through the noise. Developing a creative mindset means learning to think differently, question norms, and push boundaries.

Hold regular brainstorming sessions with your team. Encourage free thinking, and don't dismiss ideas prematurely. Even ideas that aren't immediately viable can serve as the seeds for future campaigns. Maintain an idea bank to keep track of all your creative thoughts – they might be useful down the line.

Remember, no idea is a bad idea until proven otherwise.

7. Build Strong Media Relationships

One of the most vital – and often underestimated – skills in PR is the ability to build and maintain strong relationships with the media. Understanding the media ecosystem, knowing what kind of stories different journalists cover, and respecting their time can significantly enhance your pitching success.

This skill develops over time, often with guidance from senior colleagues. Make the effort to learn about different **media beats, deadlines, and preferences**, and always personalize your communication. Respect earns trust – and trust earns coverage.

8. Understand and Leverage Social Media

Social media has emerged as a powerful extension of PR. It offers real-time engagement, broad reach, and immediate feedback. However, it's also fast-paced, unpredictable, and requires a deep understanding of both strategy and risk.

You must be **agile, alert, and creative** when using social media. Learn how to write compelling social content, monitor online conversations, manage influencer partnerships, and handle real-time crises. You can acquire these skills through online courses, on-the-job training, or mentorship.

Social media isn't just another channel – it's a dynamic platform that can shape brand perception in minutes.

9. Balance Strategy and Execution

A good PR professional must know how to **translate strategy into action**. While strategic thinking allows you to align your campaigns with broader business objectives, execution is what brings your vision to life.

You must learn to manage timelines, coordinate with cross-functional teams, monitor outcomes, and adapt your plans when needed. This balance is what separates an average campaign from an impactful one.

10. Show Professionalism and Passion

Finally, no list of skillsets is complete without emphasizing the importance of **professionalism, integrity, and passion**. PR is a fast-moving industry that often involves long hours, crisis management, and high-pressure situations. Your attitude, resilience, and hunger to learn will set you apart.

Stay curious, stay humble, and be open to feedback. PR agencies and clients are always on the lookout for **talented, energetic professionals** who bring fresh thinking to the table.

Conclusion

The PR industry is growing rapidly, and its role in brand building and reputation management is more critical than ever. Developing these skillsets – from writing and strategy to media relations and social media management – will give aspiring professionals a solid foundation for success.

What truly matters is your willingness to **learn, adapt, and evolve**. With passion, focus, and the right mindset, you can carve out a rewarding and impactful career in PR.

PART V

STRATEGY AND RESEARCH IN PR

1.

Honest Messaging and Transparency: Keys to Successful Campaigns

Public Relations as a practice in India has grown over the years, with many advertising agencies including PR services in their portfolios, besides the mushrooming of independent PR consultants to full-fledged PR agencies. Many global agencies have also set up shop to grow their business in India. Clients and brands trust and have put a lot of faith in PR for the simple reason that if you are transparent and honest in your messaging, you are in a position to build the credibility of your organisation and your brand. The age-old saying, *Honesty is the best policy*, works very strongly in the PR industry. To gain the public's trust, earned media must be fair and truthful with their audiences. The entire PR industry thrives on this and encourages brands to be authentic and transparent in whatever they are communicating.

A very honest messaging will help the brand in the long run and will also be able to build a strong bond with the media, as journalists will come forward to carry the news. With the rapid digital transformation happening today, consumers are far more intelligent, so as a brand, you need to be very careful. Consumers are looking to trust the brands they use, as it is the trust factor that makes them buy a certain kind of product or brand. With so much of personalisation happening, driving home an honest messaging will help the brand in building its equity.

In verticals like technology and automobile, most of the brands deliver very honest and clear message—especially in the case of automobiles, where the journalists take the vehicle for a long test drive and present an honest opinion on the brand of vehicle they test-ride and share their true experience. Many international brands organise fam trips for journalists to get a first-hand experience of cars and also interact with the team closely to know everything about the vehicle. Some of the well-known automobile brands also recall the vehicles when there is a serious technical defect, which is another way of being honest and transparent about the product.

Honest messaging also helps reinforce the brand image and equity, and also strengthens corporate branding. It then percolates and spreads across all other products of the company. Even in the business of advertising, they always said that one should be honest about what the product delivers and not overpromise, thereby losing the face and credibility of the brand. Delivering the right brand benefits should be the mantra when you plan your campaign, be it Advertising or PR.

Managing a consumer-facing brand always poses the challenge—if something goes wrong, the news spreads fast. We have seen this in the past with Maggi noodles and Cadbury, who had tough times when they went through a severe crisis. So today, in this digital world, brands are always very cautious in protecting their brand equity and therefore ensure that they are very transparent when it comes to messaging. It also helps in keeping a check on the health of the brand. In a category like the FMCG, since it is available across the country in all markets, care should be taken in creating messaging that is honest so that the core message planned in English comes across in the regional languages in same tone and style. Campaigns are planned today for different regions, customised and made hyperlocal, but the key here is to not deviate from your overall core message by being transparent and honest.

By being honest, you can build credibility—a requirement of earned media. Unlike in advertising, PR agencies do not pay to get their stories seen, nor do they own their stories. Journalists publish earned media articles and attach their own names to them, and they will not do so if the content is not factually accurate. So, the best is to stay honest in whatever you are communicating. Only true and genuine stories will connect well with the end audiences by building a trusted relationship. Any lack of authenticity will negatively impact the source, the medium, and the subject. By remaining honest and following the strictest moral standards and ethics, and presenting your brand as a true brand, you will only help your brand to stay healthy in the consumer's mind and remain undisturbed in the long run without much crisis to handle.

2.

Why Research Must Drive Strategic PR Campaigns

I always keep wondering how much of research one uses while developing a PR campaign. We all know research is the backbone for any brand campaign, be it Advertising or PR. While advertising uses it extensively to cull out insights, PR has not taken a deep dive into research for the messaging and PR strategy for their various campaigns. Research is still in its early stages when you think of PR. There is no separate research undertaken for PR campaigns. Invariably, the research done for advertising is leveraged by the PR team to create their campaigns. I would urge all PR consultancy firms to lay more emphasis on research to get those key insights for sharper messaging.

While the importance of research is gathering momentum for PR campaigns, in most cases there is no in-depth research undertaken. Insights based on the brainstorming and messaging workshops are, by and large, considered sufficient to craft the messages. But with so much of technology in use–like ML and AI tools–brands today are deploying these tools to do research and are able to see the benefits slowly.

Without research, public relations would not be able to present the correct picture. To get your strategy right and focused, you need a strong backing of research to work on a strategy-led PR campaign. We are now in the era of presenting transparent and authentic narrative of a brand, and this is where the presence of research will strengthen one's case.

Here are my views on how research should be leveraged and how research can give that extra push in getting your PR strategy bang on. It will also raise the bar of PR as communication tool within the overall marketing strategy of the brand.

- First and foremost, data through research will help you substantiate your case and make a strong pitch to the journalist for your story.
- In any brand communication activity, identifying your target audience is always a challenge. Research will help you understand your audience well, so you can accordingly craft your messaging.
- Research does not always mean that you need to conduct structured research. A market visit and keeping your ears to the ground can also help in gathering valuable information to formulate your PR strategy.
- Well-supported research findings will always help in building the credibility. After all, PR is all about building credibility and trust.
- The most important thing in research is that it generates tons of data, some of which may be irrelevant. This is where you need to learn the art and science of reading

between lines and using the latest technology to decipher the findings.

- One must look at research as an investment in the brand. If you need to conduct separate research for the PR campaign, do not hesitate to commission that. Always view research as a long-term asset, as some findings can become intellectual property for the brand.
- Your research will deliver the right answers if you craft it well and ask the right questions. So, framing your questions is critical when working on research.
- Ideally, a PR consultancy should have a strong research cell to work with the teams across brands and across the country. In my opinion, having a strong repository of research findings—like a Wikipedia—will help in verifying facts about brands.
- Most clients today are open to conducting research, provided it is done professionally and with well-defined objectives and purpose. This will only help you to get the desired findings and support the brand in devising a strong PR strategy.
- Research is even more important in smaller towns, where there is a shift in the behaviour as compared to that in metropolitan cities. You deal with different culture, so it is important to know the local nuances through research and develop your PR strategy.

A thorough knowledge of research methods and extensive analysis of data will allow public relations practioners to add more value to their client's business. There is no shortcut in research if you want to present a good story about your client's brand. It is research that will excite journalist to go deep and bring out eye catching stories. We should also remember: once a journalist gets from you strong research-based facts and figures you will be in his good books and that way you can strengthen and build your relationships with your journalists.

3.

Storytelling As a Business Tool in Communication

Storytelling has become an essential buzzword in recent years, especially in the fields of communication, marketing, and public relations. However, it's important to recognize that storytelling isn't a modern invention–it has been around for centuries. From ancient folklore to bedtime stories, we heard as children, stories have always played a role in shaping our imagination. Similarly, storytelling has always played a crucial role in shaping human culture and understanding. It has the power to evoke emotions, convey lessons, and create lasting memories.

As children, many of us eagerly awaited the moments when we would sit around our grandparents or parents and listen intently as they told us stories. Those narratives captured our attention, sparked our imaginations, and often taught us valuable lessons. The reason we were so drawn to those stories was because of their ability to connect with us emotionally, which made them easy to understand, memorable, and impactful. This same power of storytelling is being harnessed today, not just for entertainment, but as a vital tool in the world of business communication.

In today's fast-paced, information-saturated world, businesses face the challenge of capturing and holding the attention of their audience. Traditional methods of communication, such as simply presenting facts and figures, no longer suffice. In fact, people are bombarded with so much information daily that it becomes increasingly difficult to stand out. This is where storytelling comes into play. When a business tells a compelling story, it creates a connection with the audience, making the message more relatable and easier to understand. The beauty of storytelling lies in its ability to simplify complex concepts while still making them engaging and memorable.

In public relations, the goal is to build strong relationships with a variety of stakeholders, both internal and external. External stakeholders may include journalists, business partners, potential clients, and brand loyalists, while internal stakeholders are typically employees, who are also the brand ambassadors of the organization. Communicating with these stakeholders effectively is critical for maintaining a positive image and reputation. In this context, storytelling has emerged as one of the most effective tools for engaging and influencing these audiences. It helps humanize the brand and makes the message more relatable, which is crucial in a world where consumers are seeking authenticity and emotional connections with the brands they support.

The key to successful storytelling in business is ensuring that the message is heartfelt and genuine. If the story lacks sincerity, it will fail to resonate with the audience. A powerful story should convey emotion and a strong message. Whether it's a brand's founding story, a customer success story, or an employee's journey, it should be told with passion and authenticity. The emotional connection is what makes the story stick with the audience, creating a memorable experience that lingers long after the interaction has ended.

Storytelling can also be a tool for changing perceptions, influencing behaviours, and even altering attitudes. In the world of public relations, one of the primary objectives is to influence your target audience. Through storytelling, PR professionals can shift attitudes, build belief, and establish a deeper understanding of a product, service, or company. This is because a well-crafted story has the ability to shape the way an audience perceives a brand, much more effectively than simply presenting raw data or promotional content.

When telling a story, it's not enough to rely on emotion alone; research and factual content also play a vital role. Stories should be grounded in truth, and they should be supported by data or real-world examples that reinforce the message. This is where the combination of storytelling and research becomes particularly powerful. For instance, in public relations campaigns, you may tell the story of a brand's impact on the community, but that story should be backed by statistics, testimonials, and concrete examples that prove the brand's positive influence. Doing so not only enhances the credibility of the narrative but also strengthens the message.

Storytelling has proven to be a particularly powerful tool in the digital age, where consumers have a growing appetite for authentic content. Social media platforms, blogs, and videos all provide opportunities for brands to share their stories with a broad audience. In fact, many successful digital marketing campaigns today are built around compelling stories that engage audiences on an emotional level. In the crowded and competitive world of digital marketing, it's no longer enough for brands to just advertise products or services. To truly connect with their audiences, they must tell stories that evoke emotions and spark conversations.

One of the main advantages of storytelling in the digital landscape is its ability to cut through the noise. Today's consumers are overwhelmed with advertising and marketing messages, making it difficult for any one brand to stand out. A well-crafted story, however, has the potential to capture attention in a way that traditional advertising cannot. Stories create a narrative that audiences can relate to, and they evoke feelings and responses that make them more likely to engage with the brand. Whether it's through a touching customer testimonial, an inspiring company origin story, or a visually striking video campaign, storytelling allows brands to stand out and make a meaningful impact.

In addition to engaging audiences, storytelling helps simplify complex ideas and messages. Today, consumers are faced with an overload of information, and their attention spans are shorter than ever. Stories allow brands to communicate complex concepts in a way that is digestible and easily understood. For example, instead of listing off statistics about the effectiveness of a product, a brand might tell the story of a customer who experienced a transformative change after using the product. This not only makes the message more relatable but also allows the audience to connect with it on an emotional level, which is crucial in the digital age when people are constantly seeking genuine experiences.

Furthermore, storytelling plays a significant role in building brand loyalty. When a brand tells a compelling and authentic story, it creates a connection with its audience. Over time, this connection fosters trust and emotional investment. Consumers are more likely to remain loyal to a brand they feel emotionally connected to. A strong brand story can also encourage word-of-mouth marketing, as people are more likely to share stories that resonate with them, further expanding the brand's reach.

The advent of new technologies, particularly artificial intelligence (AI), has also transformed how businesses approach storytelling. AI-powered tools can help PR professionals analyse data, track trends, and measure campaign performance more effectively. These insights allow communicators to tailor their stories in real-time, optimizing content for specific audiences and maximizing engagement. AI can also help predict potential crises or reputational risks, enabling businesses to proactively adjust their messaging to maintain a positive image.

In conclusion, storytelling has become an indispensable tool in modern business communication. It allows brands to connect with their audiences on a deeper level, build trust, influence perceptions, and communicate complex ideas in a more relatable and engaging way. Storytelling is not just about selling a product or service; it's about building lasting relationships, inspiring action, and leaving a lasting impression. By combining emotional appeal, authenticity, and research, businesses can use storytelling to create powerful narratives that resonate with their audiences and drive success in an increasingly crowded and competitive marketplace.

4.

Value Over Volume: The Shift Toward Strategy-Led PR

In the earlier days of Public Relations (PR), success was often measured by the sheer volume of media coverage. Clients would be thrilled to exceed a targeted number of clippings for a specific campaign. The focus was on generating as much visibility as possible, with little emphasis on the quality or context of the coverage.

However, as the media landscape evolved and audiences became more discerning, the emphasis gradually shifted from quantity to quality. Today, PR is no longer just about achieving a high volume of mentions; it is about ensuring that every piece of coverage effectively conveys the intended message and reaches the right audience. This transition reflects a broader move from volume to value in PR strategy.

The Shift Towards Quality and Strategic Messaging

Modern PR focuses on crafting thoughtful, strategic campaigns that are rooted in consumer insights. The objective is not just to be seen but to make a meaningful impact. The core of this approach lies in developing relevant and strong messaging that resonates with the target audience. An effective PR strategy today is about sparking interest, engaging the core audience, and building credibility through well-substantiated communication.

For instance, instead of aiming for hundreds of generic news mentions, a modern PR campaign might prioritize getting featured in a few highly influential industry publications. This not only ensures greater relevance but also positions the brand as a voice of authority in its field. A well-placed thought leadership article or an exclusive interview in a reputed magazine can often do more for brand perception than dozens of minor mentions.

The Role of Social Media and Influencers

With the rise of social media, PR has become more dynamic and multidimensional. Social platforms enable brands to engage directly with their audiences, and influencers play a pivotal role in amplifying messages. Today, a well-strategized influencer collaboration can yield more meaningful engagement than traditional media mentions. PR professionals must therefore integrate influencer partnerships into their strategies to maintain relevance and foster authentic connections.

Influencers offer a personal touch that traditional PR methods often lack. By aligning with individuals who have a loyal following and credible voice, brands can humanize their stories and achieve deeper audience engagement. Whether through Instagram, YouTube or LinkedIn, these collaborations can effectively build brand loyalty while delivering measurable outcomes.

The Challenge of Measuring PR Effectiveness

Measurement in PR has long been a subject of debate. Traditionally, PR professionals have relied on calculating the Advertising Value Equivalent (AVE) of media coverage as a measure of success. However, this method often fails to capture the true impact of the coverage, as it does not consider factors like message resonance, sentiment, or audience engagement.

Today, more qualitative metrics are being incorporated into PR measurement frameworks. These include sentiment analysis, social media engagement rates, and the direct impact of coverage on brand perception. By analyzing these factors, PR professionals can better gauge the effectiveness of their campaigns beyond mere volume.

Real-World Example: From Quantity to Quality

Consider a tech startup launching a new product. In the past, the PR strategy might have involved securing as many mentions as possible across various news outlets. In contrast, the modern approach would focus on securing a few well-placed stories in technology-specific publications, leveraging influencers for authentic reviews, and creating interactive content that fosters community engagement.

Embracing a Value-Driven PR Approach

The PR landscape continues to evolve, with brands increasingly recognizing the importance of value-driven communication. The focus is now on crafting stories that matter, building lasting relationships with the media, and nurturing brand advocates who can amplify the message organically. As the industry

initiative honors ordinary citizens who have shown extraordinary courage in challenging situations. Over the years, this platform has gained nationwide recognition and has successfully created an emotional connection with the public.

However, the initiative is not without its contradictions. While the awards promote valour and social good, the parent brand is in the tobacco industry–a sector that faces health and ethical scrutiny. This duality raises questions: Is the company genuinely interested in promoting social causes, or is it using CSR as a shield to divert attention from its core business?

Regardless of the intent, this case illustrates how **CSR can play a strong role in building public relations**, provided it resonates with the audience and is consistent in delivery. However, it also underlines the importance of **brand-cause alignment**.

The Importance of Brand Fit in CSR Initiatives

The effectiveness of any CSR initiative is deeply linked to the **relevance of the cause to the business**. When there's a clear brand fit–where the cause aligns naturally with the brand's values, mission, and offerings–the effort is perceived as authentic. This not only strengthens the company's image but also encourages consumers to engage with and trust the brand.

For example, **Tata Group** has consistently been at the forefront of CSR in India. Their initiatives span across education, health, rural development, and environmental sustainability. What sets Tata apart is that their CSR work is deeply embedded in the group's values and culture. Through organizations like **Tata Trusts**, they have impacted millions of lives across the country, without aggressively promoting these efforts as marketing tools.

The public recognition comes as a byproduct of the genuine impact they create.

Similarly, **ITC Limited**, while operating in sectors like FMCG, agribusiness, and paperboards, has shown remarkable commitment to rural development, water stewardship, and sustainable farming. Their e-Choupal initiative has transformed the lives of farmers by providing real-time information and digital empowerment. This not only aligns with their business interests but also builds deep-rooted goodwill in rural India—a crucial market for many of ITC's products.

CSR vs Surrogate Advertising: A Thin Line

There is a growing trend of companies in **restricted categories**—such as alcohol and tobacco—using CSR as a backdoor for brand visibility. In industries where direct advertising is prohibited, brands often support social causes, events, or public service messages that indirectly highlight their name or identity.

For example, certain **liquor brands** have launched initiatives around responsible drinking, road safety, or cultural events—cleverly positioning their branding while skirting around advertising bans. While these campaigns may technically fall under CSR or cause-related marketing, they often lack depth in social commitment and are perceived as **surrogate advertising**.

This approach might deliver short-term visibility, but it risks long-term damage to brand trust, especially if consumers recognize the intent as self-serving. **CSR cannot and should not be used merely as a PR gimmick.** The credibility of the initiative hinges on its purpose, execution, and long-term impact.

Brands Getting It Right: Genuine CSR in India

Here are a few examples of Indian brands that have implemented meaningful and well-aligned CSR initiatives:

- **Mahindra Group** launched **Project Nanhi Kali**, supporting the education of underprivileged girls. As a group that values empowerment and education, this initiative beautifully complements its brand philosophy.
- **Hindustan Unilever's Project Shakti** empowers rural women entrepreneurs by training them to distribute HUL's products in their communities. It promotes gender empowerment while creating a sustainable distribution network–a win-win situation rooted in brand relevance.
- **Infosys Foundation**, led by Sudha Murty, has made significant contributions in healthcare, education, arts, and rural development. Their work is not loud or overly branded, but it has built immense goodwill for the company over the years.
- **Maruti Suzuki** has focused on road safety and driver training–perfectly aligned with their core business. Through initiatives like the **Institute of Driving and Traffic Research (IDTR)**, the company ensures safer roads while strengthening its image as a responsible automobile manufacturer.

Key Takeaways for Meaningful CSR

- **Authenticity is everything:** Consumers are increasingly discerning and can differentiate between a genuine effort and a marketing gimmick.
- **Brand-cause alignment matters:** Supporting causes that relate to your business creates stronger impact and better public reception.
- **Long-term commitment pays off:** CSR should not be seen as a campaign, but as a long-term investment in society and brand equity.
- **Avoid surrogate intent:** CSR initiatives must not be driven solely by visibility goals, especially in sectors with advertising restrictions.
- **Measure and communicate impact:** Transparency in outcomes and storytelling around real impact enhances both trust and credibility.

In conclusion, CSR offers a powerful platform to build public relations–but only when done with purpose, relevance, and sincerity. As Indian consumers become more socially aware, brands that demonstrate real commitment to social causes will not only earn respect but also build stronger, more enduring connections with their audience.

PART VI

THE NEXT IN PR: EMERGING TRENDS RESHAPING COMMUNICATION

1.

Internal Communications: Strengthening Culture from Within

Effective communication is the foundation of any successful organization. A strong internal communication strategy not only facilitates smooth operations but also energizes and motivates employees, who serve as brand ambassadors to the external world. When employees are well-informed, engaged, and aligned with company goals, they contribute more effectively to the organization's success.

Internal communication is more than just the dissemination of information; it is about fostering a culture of transparency, trust, and collaboration. It involves producing and delivering messages on behalf of leadership while also creating opportunities for meaningful dialogue across all levels of the organization. Whether it's sharing new policies, strategic goals, company milestones, or upcoming events, a well-structured communication strategy ensures that employees remain connected, informed, and engaged.

While internal communication has traditionally been managed by HR, corporate communication teams are now playing a more active role in crafting comprehensive strategies to strengthen internal engagement. According to a study by IBM, 72% of employees do not fully understand their organization's strategy, largely due to ineffective internal communication. This gap can lead to confusion, disengagement, and misalignment with business objectives. By prioritizing clear and consistent internal communication, companies can enhance employee understanding, drive productivity, and build a stronger organizational culture.

So, what are the essential elements of a successful internal communication strategy?

Establishing a Clear Flow of Communication Aligned with Strategy

Establishing a clear flow of communication aligned with strategy is crucial for ensuring information reaches employees efficiently. Structured communication channels should be defined, and messages must align with business objectives to reinforce strategic priorities. Utilizing various formats such as newsletters, digital dashboards, internal portals, and team meetings enhances accessibility. Leadership and management teams should consistently deliver messages across departments to maintain coherence.

Ensuring Transparency and Honesty

Transparency and honesty are essential in fostering a culture of trust. Sharing both successes and challenges openly helps employees stay engaged. Leadership should lead by example by being accessible and approachable while providing regular updates on company performance, decisions, and changes.

Addressing concerns proactively prevents misinformation and speculation, reinforcing credibility.

Encouraging Two-Way Communication and Feedback

Encouraging two-way communication and feedback enhances employee involvement. Open forums, surveys, and suggestion boxes allow employees to share insights, while team meetings and town halls provide platforms for discussion. Active listening and implementing constructive suggestions demonstrate a commitment to employee engagement. Recognizing contributions reinforces a culture of participation and value.

Communicating Messages with Clarity and Consistency

Messages must be communicated with clarity and consistency to ensure they are easily understood. Using simple, concise language while avoiding jargon prevents confusion. Key messages should be reinforced across multiple platforms, and communication styles should be tailored to different audiences for maximum impact.

Using Communication as a Motivational Tool

Communication can also serve as a powerful motivational tool. Celebrating achievements, milestones, and employee contributions boosts morale. Recognizing outstanding performance, sharing inspiring stories, and reinforcing the company's mission and values create a positive work environment and a sense of purpose among employees.

Building Trust and Fostering a Sense of Belonging

Building trust and fostering a sense of belonging strengthen organizational culture. Regular communication of the organization's vision, mission, and values ensures alignment. Encouraging collaboration and teamwork through shared goals, recognizing diverse perspectives, and fostering an inclusive culture make employees feel valued and respected.

Investing in Effective Training and Development

Investing in effective training and development ensures that employees and leaders are equipped with the necessary communication skills. Workshops and training sessions on best practices, resources for navigating internal communication channels, and continuous learning opportunities aligned with organizational goals enhance overall communication effectiveness.

Continuously Improving and Innovating Communication Strategies

Continuous improvement and innovation in communication strategies keep engagement levels high. Regular assessments through employee feedback and analytics help identify areas for enhancement. Leveraging technology such as AI-powered chatbots, digital workspaces, and collaboration tools ensures modern and efficient communication. Adapting to emerging trends and experimenting with new approaches maintain a dynamic and engaging communication environment.

By implementing a well-structured internal communication strategy, organizations can strengthen their culture, improve employee engagement, and drive overall business success. Prioritizing transparency, clarity, and innovation in communication ensures employees remain informed and motivated.

2.

The Rise of Public Affairs in Modern PR

Unlike their PR counterparts, public affairs practitioners concentrate on influencing public policy. Public affairs professionals working in this field aim to impact public life and policy that affects business operations and the relationship between businesses and the public. Their role often extends beyond the commercial objectives of PR, focusing instead on lawmaking and the political landscape.

These professionals work collaboratively within their organization, aligning strategies with the priorities of the business to contribute to overall success. They also:

- **Engage with Political Advisors** – Public affairs specialists maintain close relationships with political advisors, government officials, and policy influencers. This ensures that businesses are aware of upcoming policy changes and can proactively advocate for policies that benefit their industry.

- **Establish Contact with Politicians** – Building and maintaining relationships with lawmakers and legislators is crucial. This involves direct lobbying, participation in policy discussions, and contributing to legislative processes that can impact business operations.
- **Adhere to Socially Responsible Strategies** – Public affairs professionals integrate corporate social responsibility (CSR) initiatives into business strategies, ensuring that companies are not only compliant with regulations but also perceived as responsible and ethical entities. This is particularly important in India, where CSR has become a mandatory corporate practice under the Companies Act, 2013.
- **Influence Public Policy** – Through research, advocacy, and strategic communication, public affairs professionals shape public debates and influence policymakers' decisions. They use media outreach, stakeholder engagement, and grassroots movements to create a favourable environment for business interests.

Growth of Public Affairs in India

Public affairs as a practice has witnessed significant growth in India in recent years. The increasing complexity of regulatory frameworks, the government's push for economic reforms, and the rising role of multinational corporations in India's economy have all contributed to its expansion. Companies across industries, especially in sectors such as pharmaceuticals, technology, infrastructure, and finance, are investing in public affairs to navigate regulatory challenges and establish better relationships with policymakers.

The rise of digital advocacy and social media has also played a key role in shaping public opinion and government policies. Organizations are leveraging digital platforms to engage with stakeholders, mobilize public support, and drive policy conversations in real-time.

Potential of Public Affairs in a Growing Economy Like India

India's rapid economic growth, coupled with evolving government policies, creates a significant opportunity for public affairs professionals. As new policies emerge to regulate industries, businesses require expert guidance to adapt to these changes and ensure compliance while safeguarding their interests. The government's focus on initiatives such as "Make in India," "Digital India," and "Atmanirbhar Bharat" has increased the need for strategic public affairs engagements.

With India's dynamic political environment and regulatory landscape, businesses that invest in public affairs can gain a competitive advantage. The field has immense potential for growth, especially as corporations, industry associations, and non-profits recognize the need for advocacy and structured government relations.

Public Affairs on the Global Stage

Globally, public affairs have become a key component of corporate strategy. In regions such as the United States and the European Union, companies employ sophisticated lobbying and advocacy strategies to shape public policy. PR firms worldwide have expanded their services to include public affairs consulting, recognizing its importance in managing corporate reputation and policy influence.

In developed economies, public affairs professionals work extensively with think tanks, regulatory bodies, and advocacy groups to create a conducive business environment. The Indian market is gradually adopting similar practices, with PR firms increasingly offering specialized public affairs services to their clients.

Career Scope and Growth in Public Affairs

As public affairs is still in a nascent stage in India, the career scope for professionals in this field is evolving rapidly. There is a growing demand for specialists who can navigate complex policy environments, engage with government stakeholders, and drive corporate advocacy initiatives.

Public affairs professionals in India can explore diverse roles in:

- **Corporate Organizations** – Many large companies now have dedicated public affairs departments to manage government relations, compliance, and advocacy efforts.
- **Public Relations and Public Affairs Firms** – PR agencies are expanding their offerings to include public affairs, creating new career opportunities for professionals with expertise in policy advocacy and stakeholder engagement.
- **Industry Associations and Trade Bodies** – These organizations require skilled professionals to

represent their interests before policymakers and regulatory authorities.

- **Think Tanks and Policy Research Organizations** – With the growing importance of policy-driven business strategies, think tanks are hiring professionals to conduct research and engage in policy discussions.
- **Government Advisory Roles** – Experienced public affairs professionals can transition into advisory roles, assisting policymakers in shaping regulations that balance industry growth and public interest.

With India's regulatory landscape continuously evolving, the demand for skilled public affairs professionals is expected to rise. Those with expertise in policy analysis, strategic communication, and government relations will find significant career growth and leadership opportunities in this domain.

Do Clients Entrust PR Agencies for Public Affairs or Manage It Internally?

The approach to managing public affairs varies across organizations and industries. While some companies prefer to build internal teams to handle government relations and policy advocacy, others rely on specialized PR agencies to provide public affairs services.

- **In-House Public Affairs Teams** – Large corporations, particularly those in highly regulated sectors like pharmaceuticals, telecom, and infrastructure, often establish dedicated public affairs departments. These teams have direct engagement with policymakers, regulatory bodies, and industry stakeholders, ensuring a consistent and long-term advocacy strategy.

- **PR and Public Affairs Agencies** – Many companies, especially mid-sized and multinational firms entering new markets, turn to PR agencies with public affairs expertise. These agencies bring strategic counsel, industry connections, and specialized skills in lobbying, crisis management, and policy advocacy. PR firms also provide an external perspective and access to a broader network of policymakers and media influencers.
- **Hybrid Approach** – Some businesses adopt a hybrid model where an internal team oversees overall public affairs strategy while partnering with external agencies for execution, media outreach, and specific policy campaigns.

The choice between in-house and agency-led public affairs efforts depends on factors such as industry regulations, budget, company size, and the complexity of the policy environment. In India, as public affairs continues to evolve, an increasing number of PR firms are expanding their capabilities to offer government relations and advocacy services, making them a valuable partner for businesses navigating the regulatory landscape.

3.

Embracing PR While Tackling Talent and Content Challenges

More brands will embrace PR in the future. However, it will always be a challenge for agencies in today's digital world to meet modern client expectations.

PR had enough struggle for both respectability and clarity of purpose, but the industry has overcome that today and every brand is very closely embracing PR as an important communication tool when they draw their overall marketing plan for their company and their respective brands.

Clients must be now more open to exploring new avenues in PR and will be looking at more innovative ways to explore Public Relations, especially in today's digital world.

The year 2023 saw greater openness and an increased embrace of brands utilizing PR. Looking ahead, this trend is likely to encourage more clients to closely examine and incorporate PR into their annual marketing plans.

I feel, we may not see any major shift in next two years as some of the challenges in the area of talent and content creation will continue to bother the industry. Agencies will have to beef up their technology set-up and operations with the right talent.

Many start-ups, which depended a lot on PR, played very carefully in 2023 as there was not enough budget to look at PR and promotions. With start-ups still finding their footing, we may still see start-ups using PR but more diligently and judiciously. Where PR was concerned, most startup verticals revisited their strategy to ensure it proposed a view of moderation rather than going full hog.

Data and insights will play a major role and will be very critical in drawing forceful PR strategies. Innovation and strategic storytelling, with strong narratives backed by technology, will help in crafting very focussed messaging.

This is where we may see the role of ML and AI coming into play, to help in leveraging the data used more intelligently. So, technology will be crucial for agencies to gear up and get their talent in place to meet the client demands. Clients will expect more insights, sharp messaging, and data-driven audience profiling to reach the right audiences.

The years 2023 and 2024 also saw several good IPOs, where Corporate and financial PR had a major role to play and agencies who are specialists in this area played a significant role and there will be more opportunities in the coming year.

With the wind still moving in the positive direction as far as the economy is concerned it will help in bringing stability in the financial market and a better investment climate for both the institutions and retail investors and we could see more action on the corporate and financial PR in the future.

The recent election wins in three major states by the ruling party have also boosted the confidence of many industries more from the stability point of view. These election wins have brought in a strong foundation to have a strong and stable government at the centre. With reforms moving in the right direction, we can expect industries to be bullish and optimistic for better growth in the new financial year.

On the PR agencies front, we have not seen any major takeovers from the international PR networks. A few happened, but it looks like new network agencies entering India have slowed down.

On the contrary, the local PR agencies are now shining better and are in the limelight by offering new services and trying to be more innovative and technologically equally advanced, especially in the digital space, which is going to be an architect for many social media-led campaigns. With new guidelines being framed for influencer campaigns etc. by the ASCI, the credibility of influencer campaigns should go up considerably.

One important change that can be foreseen is the role of the CEOs and MDs in seriously looking at corporate reputation. Reputation is going to be very crucial and pivotal for every organisation as the advent of social media and fake news are becoming very sensitive in today's corporate world.

So, CEOs and MDs will closely work and monitor with the corporate communication team on reputation management continuously. So, in a VUCA world, the agility and alertness to avert any crisis will be paramount for brands to have a robust communication team to fight and manage crises.

Overall, from a PR perspective, it will be a great time for the PR profession as the industry is heading towards the right growth path. Having said that agencies who can be more creative and innovative with good backing in technology will be able to drive the needs of the client in today's fast-paced digital world.

The dynamics of PR have changed and will keep changing and those who adapt to the quick change will be able to manage brands and grow their business. This coming year will also be the year for learning new technology and therefore investments in training and development will have to be made by agencies to upskill their talent across the board.

4.

Corporate Communications: A Strategic Business Function

Corporate communications have gained significant momentum over the last decade. Many professionals who start their careers in PR agencies often aspire to transition to the client side, where they can oversee corporate communication strategies and manage agencies instead of executing campaigns themselves. However, the reality is that excelling in corporate communication requires a unique skill set, as it involves managing the reputation of an entire organization and engaging with multiple stakeholders. Unlike agency roles, where interactions are mostly limited to clients, corporate communication professionals must handle media, investors, employees, regulatory bodies, and the public. In today's fast-paced digital world, where news spreads in real time, maintaining a company's reputation has never been more crucial.

The Increasing Focus on Corporate Communication

Today, even CEOs are deeply invested in the reputation and public image of their organizations. Corporate leaders understand that trust, credibility, and goodwill play a significant role in a company's long-term success. As a result, corporate communication professionals need to be sharp, savvy, and agile in their approach. Organizations are dedicating more resources to build their reputation, brand equity, and image, recognizing that a well-managed corporate narrative can positively influence stakeholder perceptions.

Furthermore, the rapid advancements in technology have made it imperative for corporate communication teams to stay updated with the latest digital tools and strategies. Social media, artificial intelligence, and data analytics have transformed the way companies communicate and manage their reputation. Professionals in this field must be adept at crisis communication, brand storytelling, and proactive reputation management. Additionally, the accountability of corporate communication professionals has increased, as they work closely with the CEO's office and dynamic leadership teams to craft messaging that aligns with business goals.

The Growing Demand for Corporate Communication Professionals

With companies seeking rapid growth and aiming for IPOs, the demand for skilled corporate communication professionals is rising. Effective communication is essential to attract investors, assure regulators, and maintain transparency with stakeholders. Given this trend, it is likely that we will soon see specialized courses and academic programs focusing on corporate communication to train professionals for this critical function.

Key Reasons Why Corporate Communication is Essential

- **Establishing Dedicated Corporate Communication Teams:** Many organizations are now setting up in-house corporate communication teams to take control of their brand narratives. Having a dedicated team ensures that messaging remains consistent across different platforms and that the company is prepared to handle both opportunities and crises effectively.
- **Enhancing Coordination with PR Consultants:** Corporate communication teams act as a bridge between organizations and external PR agencies. They ensure that agencies understand the company's vision, goals, and key messaging while aligning media outreach strategies accordingly. This coordination leads to more effective communication and better results from PR efforts.
- **Building Stronger Relationships with Journalists and Media Houses:** Media relations are a crucial part of corporate communication. By maintaining healthy relationships with journalists, corporate communicators ensure that accurate information about the company is conveyed to the public. A well-managed media strategy helps in shaping a positive brand image and mitigating potential misinformation.
- **Protecting Corporate Reputation Through Continuous Monitoring:** Reputation management is one of the core responsibilities of corporate

communication teams. With the prevalence of social media and online news platforms, any negative news or crisis can escalate quickly. Continuous monitoring of public sentiment, media coverage, and online discussions allows companies to respond proactively, protecting their image and credibility.

- **Strengthening Internal Communication and Employee Engagement**: Corporate communication is not just about external messaging; internal communication plays a vital role in fostering a strong organizational culture. Transparent and effective communication within a company enhances employee morale, aligns teams with business objectives, and builds a sense of trust and belonging among the workforce.
- **Supporting Investor Relations and Financial Communication**: Companies planning to go public or seeking investments must maintain clear and transparent communication with stakeholders. Corporate communication professionals play a pivotal role in crafting investor presentations, financial reports, and regulatory disclosures, ensuring that the company maintains trust and compliance with industry standards.
- **Crisis Management and Damage Control**: In today's volatile business environment, crises can arise unexpectedly. Whether it's a product recall, legal dispute, or public backlash, a strong corporate communication team is essential in managing crises effectively. Having a well-prepared crisis communication

strategy helps in minimizing damage and restoring stakeholder confidence.

- **Leveraging Digital Media for Brand Storytelling**: The digital landscape has transformed corporate communication. Companies now leverage social media, blogs, podcasts, and video content to narrate their brand story authentically. A strategic approach to digital communication helps organizations connect with audiences on a deeper level and humanize their brand.

Conclusion

Corporate communication is no longer a supplementary function—it is a strategic imperative for businesses aiming to thrive in a competitive and rapidly evolving marketplace. Companies that invest in strong corporate communication teams not only safeguard their reputation but also build stronger relationships with stakeholders, enhance brand trust, and create long-term business value. As the corporate world continues to evolve, professionals in this domain must continually upgrade their skills, stay ahead of industry trends, and embrace innovation in communication strategies.

5.
The Chief Communications Officer: From Manager to Strategic Leader

The role of communication in organizations has undergone a significant transformation over the past decade. In the early days, communication was often seen as a one-way street, where messages were pushed out to employees and stakeholders through traditional methods like newsletters and occasional media coverage. However, as the media landscape has evolved and the business environment has become more volatile, uncertain, complex, and ambiguous (VUCA), the role of the Chief Communications Officer (CCO) has become indispensable.

Today, the CCO is not just a gatekeeper of information but a strategic leader responsible for managing corporate reputation, handling crises, and aligning communication strategies with the organization's business objectives. The significance of corporate communication has increased manifold, making the CCO a vital part of the senior leadership team.

The Transformation of the CCO Role

In the past, corporate communication was predominantly managed by the PR department. The primary focus was on securing media coverage and circulating internal newsletters. These newsletters often faced challenges related to timely content collection and distribution. Moreover, communication was largely unidirectional, with limited engagement or feedback mechanisms.

Today, the CCO's role is far more dynamic. It involves not only maintaining a positive corporate image but also proactively addressing potential risks and crises. With the rise of social media and the digital landscape, communication has shifted from a monologue to a dialogue, requiring real-time engagement with multiple stakeholders.

The Strategic Importance of CCOs

CCOs now play a pivotal role in ensuring the stability and enhancement of a company's reputation. Organizations increasingly recognize the need for a robust communication strategy that aligns with overall business goals. As a result, CEOs and boards are investing in experienced communication leaders who can seamlessly integrate communication efforts across functions.

One of the most critical aspects of the CCO's role today is managing the thin line between marketing and communication. While marketing focuses on promoting products and services, communication builds the brand's ethos, values, and reputation. Bridging this gap ensures that brand messaging remains consistent across all touchpoints.

Key Responsibilities of the Modern CCO

- **Reputation Management:** CEOs now prioritize hiring competent CCOs because corporate reputation significantly impacts business success. A strong reputation attracts talent, fosters stakeholder trust, and enhances brand credibility.
- **Strengthening Internal Communication:** CCOs work closely with Chief Human Resource Officers (CHROs) to ensure cohesive internal messaging. This collaboration fosters a unified communication strategy that resonates with all employees.
- **Collaboration with Leadership:** Effective communication requires alignment with the CEO and the senior leadership team. A well-integrated approach helps in quicker decision-making and streamlined messaging.
- **Navigating the VUCA World:** In a rapidly changing environment, CCOs must stay agile and prepared for crises. The COVID-19 pandemic underscored the need for adaptive communication strategies, emphasizing transparency and empathy.
- **Budget Management:** Though communication departments are often seen as cost centres, CCOs must demonstrate the value of their initiatives. They are responsible for managing budgets effectively, ensuring that every campaign delivers measurable outcomes.
- **Leveraging Data and Technology:** Modern communication strategies are data-driven. By analyzing

stakeholder sentiments and digital engagement metrics, CCOs can craft more targeted messages.

- **Performance Measurement:** It is crucial for CCOs to evaluate the impact of their communication initiatives. Implementing key performance indicators (KPIs) and feedback mechanisms helps in assessing the effectiveness of campaigns.
- **Employee Engagement and Advocacy:** CCOs play a crucial role in fostering employee advocacy. By creating strong internal communication channels and encouraging employees to become brand ambassadors, they build a positive organizational culture.
- **Crisis Communication Planning:** Developing a robust crisis communication plan ensures that organizations can respond swiftly and efficiently during emergencies. This planning minimizes damage and preserves reputation.
- **Social Responsibility and Sustainability Communication:** CCOs increasingly focus on communicating the company's commitment to sustainability and social responsibility. Transparent communication on these issues fosters stakeholder trust.

The Future of Corporate Communication

As the role of the CCO continues to evolve, companies are increasingly involving them in strategic business decisions. By integrating communication with business strategy, CCOs can contribute to long-term value creation.

Moreover, as organizations embrace digital transformation, CCOs must remain at the forefront of innovation. They should foster a culture of agility, where communication professionals are well-versed in the latest digital tools and platforms.

The future also demands that CCOs advocate for ethical communication practices, maintaining transparency and authenticity in an age where misinformation can quickly go viral. They must build resilience into their communication strategies to withstand challenges posed by new media landscapes.

Conclusion

The role of the Chief Communications Officer has transformed from that of a traditional PR manager to a strategic leader. As organizations navigate the complexities of the VUCA world, CCOs must continuously adapt, leveraging data, collaboration, and agile strategies to protect and enhance brand reputation. CEOs and business leaders should view communication as an integral part of the business strategy rather than a peripheral function. By doing so, they can fully harness the CCO's potential to build a resilient and reputable organization. As the business world continues to evolve, the importance of strategic communication will only grow, making the CCO's role indispensable in shaping corporate success.

6.

The Strategic Alliance of PR And Branding

In today's fast-paced, highly competitive business landscape, branding has become more than just a marketing buzzword—it's a critical pillar of success. Whether you're a multinational corporation or an individual building a personal brand, the image you project can significantly influence your trajectory. But here's a secret that seasoned marketers know well: **branding doesn't thrive in isolation**. It needs a voice, a vehicle, and a strategy to amplify it—and that's where **Public Relations** comes into play.

Branding defines *who you are*. PR tells the *world who you are*—authentically, strategically, and compellingly. Think of branding as your personality and PR as your storytelling. When done right, PR becomes a powerful lever for building and sustaining a strong brand—both corporate and personal.

Let's break it down and explore how this synergy works in practice.

1. PR Builds Credibility for Branding

Branding without credibility is like a fancy storefront with no substance behind it. Consumers today are sceptical, research-driven, and trust-savvy. They're no longer swayed solely by clever ads; they want to see real proof that your brand delivers what it promises.

This is where PR shines. Through media coverage, thought leadership articles, influencer endorsements, and third-party validations, PR **gives your brand the credibility** it needs to stand out. Unlike advertising, which is paid and perceived as biased, PR is often earned and considered more trustworthy. When a well-known journalist or influencer features your brand, it sends a signal: *This brand is worth paying attention to.*

Take, for example, a startup trying to enter a crowded market. A strong PR campaign that places the founder on podcasts, gets the product featured in reputable publications, and tells an authentic backstory can do more for brand trust than any ad spends in the early stages.

2. You Need Patience in PR as Branding Through PR Is a Long Process

Here's the hard truth: PR isn't magic, and branding isn't instant. You won't go viral overnight, and you shouldn't try to. Building a brand through PR requires **time, persistence, and consistency**.

A common mistake companies and individuals make is expecting immediate returns. They issue one press release or land one media feature and then wonder why brand awareness hasn't skyrocketed. But PR is a **slow burn**. It's about building relationships with the media, growing your presence steadily, and reinforcing your brand message over time.

Think of branding via PR like planting a tree. The first few months might not show much, but beneath the surface, roots are growing. Over time, those efforts compound–and suddenly, people start recognizing your name, understanding your values, and trusting your brand.

3. In Today's Digital World, Managing Branding Through PR Is a Huge Challenge

We're living in an era of information overload. With social media, 24/7 news cycles, online reviews, and user-generated content, your brand is constantly being shaped by conversations–some of which you have little control over. In this environment, **managing brand reputation through PR is more important–and more difficult–than ever before.**

Digital PR now requires juggling multiple platforms: social media, online publications, podcasts, YouTube, blogs, and even Reddit threads. It also means being **proactive and reactive–** crafting compelling stories, while staying prepared to manage any negative sentiment or crises in real time.

Today, the challenge isn't just about getting noticed; it's about staying relevant, protecting your reputation, and making sure your brand story is consistent across every touchpoint. That takes finesse, speed, and a deep understanding of both digital trends and human psychology.

4. You Need to Work on a Strong Strategy to Build Branding Through PR

PR without strategy is like sailing without a compass—you might move, but you won't reach your destination. A solid PR strategy for branding isn't just about getting media coverage; it's about getting the **right kind of coverage, in the right places, with the right message**.

Before you begin, ask:

- What are the core values of our brand?
- Who is our audience, and where do they consume content?
- What are our key messages and unique selling points?
- What's the tone and voice we want to maintain?
- What does success look like?

A strategic approach aligns PR activities with business and branding goals. It helps identify storytelling opportunities that highlight your brand's identity—whether it's innovation, heritage, sustainability, or community impact.

Moreover, a strong strategy makes it easier to respond to challenges. If a crisis hits or misinformation spreads, a well-planned PR framework helps you respond in a way that **preserves and protects your brand's integrity**.

5. Branding Through PR Requires Long-Term Thinking

We live in a world obsessed with short-term wins: likes, shares, clicks, sales. But branding is a **long game**, and PR plays a crucial role in that journey. It helps **build reputation equity**, which may not immediately translate to revenue but will create lasting value.

Think of iconic brands–Apple, Nike, Tesla. Their brands weren't built in a quarter; they were built over years of consistent messaging, storytelling, and public engagement. PR helped them navigate controversy, shape public perception, and stay top of mind.

For smaller businesses or individuals, long-term PR means consistently putting out expert insights, participating in meaningful industry conversations, supporting causes, and being visible in ways that align with brand values. Over time, this positions you not just as a brand–but as a leader in your space.

6. You Can Enhance and Increase Trust Through PR for Branding

At its core, branding is about **trust**–and trust is earned. PR gives your brand the tools to **communicate transparently, respond authentically, and engage meaningfully** with your audience.

Trust grows when people hear real stories, see consistent values, and observe how a brand handles both wins and challenges. PR allows you to show the human side of your brand: the people behind the scenes, the values you uphold, the causes you support, and the way you treat your customers.

Especially in the digital age, where misinformation and scepticism is high, **trust is the currency**. And PR is the bank that helps you build and protect that currency.

In Summary

Branding and PR are not just connected–they're inseparable. Branding gives you identity. PR gives you visibility, credibility, and voice. Together, they create a reputation that can withstand market shifts, consumer expectations, and digital chaos.

Whether you're a startup founder trying to make your mark, a large company reinventing your image, or a professional building a personal brand—**investing in strategic PR is one of the smartest ways to build a brand that lasts.**

So be patient, be consistent, be authentic—and let PR do what it does best: tell your story in a way the world will not only hear but believe.

7.

Planning In PR: An Evolving Function

In the advertising world, account planning is a well-established, mission-critical function. It is the unseen engine that powers human relevance, creative excellence, and strategic sharpness in campaigns. Every creative idea, media plan, and brand strategy is rooted in the planner's ability to distil human truths and cultural insights.

In contrast, the public relations (PR) industry–despite its rapid evolution–still lacks a clearly defined, independent planning function. Yet, in a world where reputation is shaped by real-time conversations, cultural trends, and earned influence, the need for structured planning in PR has never been more urgent.

As PR moves from tactical publicity to strategic brand-building, the industry must seriously ask: Where is the planning function, and why is it still missing?

1. Planning in PR: Present but Unstructured

Unlike advertising agencies, PR firms have not institutionalized planning as a standalone discipline. Some large agencies have strategy teams focused on reputation management, corporate communication, or crisis advisory. However, deep human-centered planning—based on behavioural insights, cultural mapping, and emotional drivers—is rare.

PR agencies historically grew from media relations roots, focusing on securing earned media through relationships and storytelling. Strategy was often secondary to execution. As a result, planning tends to be scattered across functions rather than organized into a dedicated, rigorous process.

Today, a handful of progressive PR firms are beginning to embed planning roles – but industry-wide, it remains a nascent, underdeveloped function.

2. How Campaign Planning Happens Today

In the absence of formal planners, PR strategy largely rests with account teams. Account managers and senior executives, who are responsible for client servicing, media relations, content development, and event management, also attempt to craft strategic direction.

Planning today often involves:

- Desk research to identify media trends.
- Social listening reports to capture conversation sentiment.
- Brainstorming sessions for campaign themes or story hooks.
- Leveraging journalist feedback to shape messaging.

While these efforts produce useful insights, they rarely achieve the depth or originality that a dedicated planner would bring. Instead of uncovering powerful human truths, campaigns often chase media-friendly narratives – quick wins that may not build long-term brand equity.

3. Drowning in Data, Starving for Insight

Modern PR firms have access to enormous datasets: real-time social conversations, media analytics, search behaviours, cultural trend reports, and influencer metrics. However, having data is not the same as using it meaningfully.

Too often, data is deployed for reporting – counting impressions, measuring sentiment, or tracking coverage. Very little is used to *inform and shape* creative strategy before a campaign even begins.

Without structured planning, PR agencies miss the opportunity to:

- Predict emerging societal and cultural trends.
- Tap into emotional drivers that move audiences.
- Identify white spaces for brand positioning.
- Build narratives that align with deep-seated human needs.

By failing to connect the dots between data and human insight, many PR campaigns risk becoming reactive, opportunistic, and ultimately forgettable.

4. Is Building a Planning Team a Cost or an Investment?

For many PR agencies, the idea of hiring a dedicated planning team raises concerns about cost structures. Margins in PR are traditionally thinner than in advertising, making additional headcount a sensitive issue.

However, building a planning function should be seen as a strategic investment, not an expense.

A strong planning team can:

- Help agencies win larger, more strategic mandates.
- Enable the creation of distinctive, high-impact campaigns.
- Deepen client relationships through smarter insights and foresight.
- Attract top creative talent seeking meaningful, insight-driven work.

Moreover, strategic campaigns anchored in human truths are more likely to deliver measurable business outcomes – making it easier for PR firms to move upstream with clients into boardroom conversations.

The return on investment for planning, when done correctly, is not just positive – it can be transformational.

5. Account Teams are Overloaded, Not Equipped for Planning

Today's PR account teams are under immense pressure. They are expected to manage daily client needs, drive media outreach, coordinate with creative and digital teams, handle crises, and deliver results – often across multiple time zones and sectors.

Adding deep strategic planning to this workload is neither realistic nor fair.

Moreover, the skills needed for world-class planning – analytical thinking, cultural decoding, behavioural insight mining, creative provocation – are distinct from the operational excellence needed for account management.

By separating the functions, agencies can allow account teams to focus on executional brilliance while empowering planners to think deeply, explore widely, and uncover the emotional and cultural drivers that should power communications strategies.

The result: Smarter, sharper, and more effective campaigns that truly connect with audiences.

6. AI and Machine Learning: Tools, Not Replacements

AI and machine learning are beginning to reshape how agencies approach data, insights, and trend prediction. Tools like Cision Insights, Meltwater, Talkwalker, Brandwatch, Pulsar, and Sprinklr allow agencies to:

- Monitor real-time conversations.
- Predict narrative shifts and emerging crises.
- Identify new influencers and advocacy networks.
- Map sentiment evolution across topics and geographies.

However, AI can only **find patterns**–it cannot **find meaning**.

Interpreting what the data reveals about human emotions, societal tensions, or cultural aspirations still requires human planners. Only humans can understand nuance, context, irony, and contradiction–all essential elements in earned storytelling.

In the future, the most successful PR planning functions will blend AI-driven speed and scale with human-driven empathy and interpretation.

Conclusion: Planning Must Power the Future of PR

The PR industry is evolving from media-focused publicity to strategic brand storytelling. As clients demand more strategic partnership, and as earned reputation becomes harder to shape and sustain, PR agencies must rethink how they approach planning.

Building a dedicated planning function is not optional—it is mission-critical.

Planners in PR must be:

- Cultural anthropologists who decode societal shifts.
- Behavioural economists who understand human decision-making.
- Data interpreters who find meaning in complexity.
- Creative catalysts who provoke new ways of storytelling.

The opportunity is clear: PR agencies that embed true strategic planning into their DNA will not only craft better campaigns—they will become trusted advisors to brands navigating an increasingly complex, fragmented, and emotional world.

The future of PR is insight-driven, human-centered, and strategically led.

And planning will be the engine that powers it.

8.

The Power of Storytelling: Crafting Narratives That Resonate

In an era where audiences are overwhelmed with information and bombarded by ads, the ability to tell a compelling story has become one of the most powerful tools in the public relations (PR) toolkit. Storytelling humanizes your brand, evokes emotions, and builds authentic connections—far beyond what traditional advertising can achieve.

According to a Nielsen study, 92% of consumers trust earned media, such as PR-driven stories, over paid advertisements. This staggering figure underscores the growing importance of crafting meaningful narratives to shape perceptions and drive engagement. Let's explore why storytelling is not just an option, but a necessity for effective PR, and how you can harness its full potential.

Why Storytelling is an Essential Tool in PR

At its core, PR is about communication and connection. Storytelling provides the emotional thread that ties together facts, figures, and corporate messaging into something memorable and impactful.

When you tell a story—especially one that feels personal and authentic—you're not just relaying information. You're taking your audience on a journey. You're helping them feel your values, understand your purpose, and remember your message. Whether you're announcing a new product, responding to a crisis, or building thought leadership, stories give depth to your communication and make it resonate.

Here's how storytelling transforms PR into a force that captures hearts and minds:

1. Stories Build Trust and Emotional Connections

People don't trust brands—they trust people. And people tell stories.

When a narrative is told with sincerity and depth, it humanizes your organization. Audiences begin to see the people behind the brand. They relate to your struggles, values, and wins. Whether it's a founder's journey, a behind-the-scenes look at your team, or a customer success story, these narratives inspire confidence and loyalty.

Stories tap into emotions—curiosity, empathy, excitement, or hope—which are far more powerful than a press release packed with stats. Emotions drive action, and trust is the foundation of long-term brand loyalty.

2. Thought Leaders Use Stories to Drive Influence

A good thought leader doesn't just present data—they tell stories that make their message stick.

When leaders speak through anecdotes, metaphors, and personal experiences, they transform abstract ideas into digestible, memorable content. This storytelling prowess helps them stand out in a sea of sameness, especially in industries where expertise can be technical or dry.

Public relations professionals can use storytelling to position executives and spokespeople as trusted voices. Sharing stories of lessons learned, industry insights, or visionary thinking helps establish authority while remaining relatable and real.

3. Storytelling Allows You to Express Your Creative Strengths

PR is no longer limited to press releases and media outreach. It now encompasses content marketing, social media, video, podcasts, and more. Storytelling gives PR professionals a chance to flex their creative muscles and craft narratives across multiple formats.

You can use stories to:

- Bring data to life in an infographic.
- Create an emotional connection through a short video.
- Spark conversations with behind-the-scenes posts on social media.
- Capture attention in a pitch that leads with a compelling human-interest angle.

Creativity is the differentiator in today's crowded media landscape, and storytelling is its canvas.

4. Great Stories are Memorable and Shareable

Facts are easy to forget, but stories linger in the mind. Just think about your favourite TED Talk—it probably started with a powerful story, not a slide of bullet points.

In PR, storytelling ensures your message sticks long after the audience walks away. A good story creates a mental image and an emotional imprint, which increases recall. It also enhances shareability, encouraging media outlets, influencers, and the public to pass it along.

This is especially important in today's attention economy, where the average consumer scrolls through hundreds of messages a day. A memorable story cuts through the noise and stays top of mind.

5. Storytelling is More Than a Marketing Tool—It's a Strategic Asset

It's easy to think of storytelling as a component of marketing—but in PR, it's a strategic pillar.

Storytelling can:

- Shape your brand identity
- Manage your reputation
- Frame your response in a crisis
- Influence stakeholder perceptions
- Win community support
- Drive social change

A well-thought-out narrative helps align internal teams, external audiences, and media messaging. It acts as a guidepost for consistent communication and strengthens the overall voice of your organization.

In times of crisis or change, having a solid narrative can also help maintain control and provide clarity in moments of confusion.

6. Storytelling Helps You Reach and Engage Larger Audiences in the Digital Age

In today's digital-first world, content is king—but storytelling is its crown.

People are consuming stories on Instagram reels, LinkedIn articles, YouTube videos, newsletters, podcasts, and even tweets. A well-crafted story can be adapted and repurposed across all these channels, reaching different demographics with the same emotional impact.

Social media algorithms also favour content that generates engagement, and nothing invites more interaction than a good story. Whether it's likes, shares, comments, or mentions—stories drive conversation.

And in PR, conversation equals visibility.

How to Start Crafting Better Stories in PR

- **Know Your Audience:** Understand their interests, pain points, and what motivates them.
- **Find the Human Angle:** Focus on people—founders, customers, team members—not just products or services.
- **Be Authentic:** Audiences can smell inauthenticity. Tell real stories, even if they involve vulnerability or imperfection.

- **Use Structure:** Every story needs a beginning, middle, and end. Hook the audience, build tension, and end with resolution.
- **Incorporate Data:** Combine the power of emotion with the credibility of numbers for maximum impact.
- **Adapt for Channels:** One story can live in many forms. Tailor it for social, print, video, and podcasts accordingly.

Final Thoughts

Storytelling isn't just a buzzword—it's the backbone of modern PR. It helps brands build trust, drive engagement, and make meaningful connections. It turns information into emotion, statistics into stories, and companies into causes people care about.

As attention spans shrink and scepticism grows, those who can craft and tell great stories will lead the narrative—and ultimately, win the hearts of their audience.

So, the next time you're crafting a PR strategy, ask yourself: *What's the story I want the world to hear?*

PART VII

THE NEXT WAVE OF PR IN INDIA

1.

From Data To AI: The PR Playbook For 2025

From AI-driven messaging to influencer marketing, 2025 will see PR embracing tech and data like never before, redefining how brands tell their stories.

Today, every brand and corporation recognise the value of PR. With the cost of media going up, brands are prudently looking at PR as a tool to create visibility for themselves. More than just increasing visibility, they are also keen to establish a credible image for their brand.

Brands are eager to cultivate their reputation and craft captivating narratives to effectively engage their audience. As we transition into 2025, new trends will emerge as consumer behaviour and technological advancements present new opportunities for brands to communicate more transparently and authentically.

Influencers will play a significant role, but brands must carefully plan their influencer selection to avoid negative publicity. Here are some of the trends one will notice as we embark on the new year:

AI in the Spotlight

There is enough going on with artificial intelligence. It was a buzzword for some time, but that has now faded, and AI is being used as a powerful tool to make communication for sharper messaging with creative thinking. We also need to understand that AI is just another tool.

At the end of the day, you need to have ideas and the right inputs for AI to deliver results. We may see more application of AI in the PR world, where brands will use it for targeted communication and predictive analytics.

It will also enhance its role in crisis communication in today's digital world where news travels fast and brands get trolled quickly.

Data-driven Storytelling

The use of data will be leveraged to the maximum, especially the first-party data. A good amount of data with the right tools will help you cull out interesting insights to work on your messaging and the narratives that you want to tell your audience.

Content we know has always been a challenge, but with so much data available, and if investments are made in the right tools to manage the data, brands can curate a lot of fresh content, which will help in engaging with your target audience.

Talent Crunch and Industry Challenges

The story of resource crunch will continue. The generation today has different expectations when it comes to work. They just do not want to do the mundane work, especially the freshers who want to catapult to more responsibility in a matter of one year.

Not only that, but clients are also eager to adopt the latest tools and embrace innovative thinking. Meanwhile, the corporate communications field is expanding rapidly, with many young executives making the switch–resulting in a growing talent crisis within agencies.

Also, the pressures in agencies to meet tight deadlines are not liked by many employees today, which is what frustrates many to quickly jump to a cooler place where some of them sacrifice their monetary compensation to have a balanced lifestyle of work.

Business Dynamics

Business movements will happen, but generally in the PR business, clients never try to disturb the relationships with their PR partners if the going is good. A few pitches will happen across various categories, but the internationally affiliated agencies will benefit from the global alignments when these international clients launch their products in India.

A lot of new agencies will make specific efforts to do some cold calls, but my vast experience says that cold calls never work when it comes to new business.

Most business comes through strong referrals. And there are agencies that are very careful in choosing and going after new business, as there is not enough talent available to manage the existing business, so the question of new business will be viewed with a lot of caution. And agencies here need to be well equipped with the latest technology and skillsets to meet their client expectations.

Influencers: The New Brand Ambassadors

The role of influencers as important brand ambassadors is already gathering momentum as more brands are carefully aligning with the right influencers. Today brands are inclined towards influencer marketing as an effective PR tool, with a majority of Indian brands opting for influencers and content creators as a part of their marketing mix.

In the year 2025 we could see more micro-influencers stepping in, and brands will use them with greater depth and engagement with their audiences. An influencer with good credentials will always add credibility to the brands as they are more transparent and genuine. Today, most consumers trust the word of influencers if they come with a good background and credentials. Hence, I would see more brand engagement through influencers.

Authenticity is Key

The brands must stay authentic and transparent in all their communication. Don't try to brush anything under the carpet if something has gone wrong with your product or service. Be honest and positive so that brands can be shielded and protected from being diluted further.

The trends may not drastically change from what we saw in 2024, but new trends will emerge in 2025, especially in the digital world, where we can expect hyper-targeted communication to play a vital role. Agencies should also up their budget to impart more intense training, as new communication tools will play an active role in deciphering data and use of data for sharper insights and focused communication.

2.

From Press Releases to Instagram Reels: How Influencers Have Redefined Public Relations

The public relations industry has undergone a dramatic transformation over the last decade. Once anchored in traditional media relations and earned coverage, PR has evolved into a multifaceted discipline shaped heavily by the rise of digital platforms and the powerful voices of influencers. This shift has not only broadened the scope of PR but also blurred the lines between earned, owned, and paid media. Today, influencers are not just brand promoters–they're key players in strategic communication, brand perception, and audience engagement.

1. PR Hasn't Taken a Backseat–It's Expanded

With the growing dominance of influencers, some have speculated that PR has taken a secondary role. That couldn't be further from the truth. What has happened is not a displacement, but an evolution.

PR is no longer confined to press releases and journalist pitches. It now encompasses a strategic mix of content creation, digital storytelling, social media engagement, and influencer collaboration. Influencers have become valuable partners in amplifying a brand's voice and humanizing its message.

Where traditional PR built credibility through journalistic validation, modern PR leverages authenticity and relatability through influencer partnerships. This convergence means that PR has adapted, becoming more dynamic, agile, and impactful than ever before.

2. Blurring the Boundaries Between Earned and Paid Media

Historically, PR was synonymous with earned media–coverage you don't pay for but receive based on merit, relationships, and newsworthiness. Influencer marketing, however, is typically a paid form of communication. This raises an important question: Does paid influencer content belong in the PR domain?

The answer lies in how the influencer relationship is managed. Many PR professionals now curate and oversee influencer partnerships, ensuring that the messaging aligns with broader communication goals. Even when influencers are paid, the campaign's success hinges on authentic engagement and reputation building–hallmarks of PR.

Thus, while influencer marketing may originate from a paid media model, it has become an integrated extension of PR, particularly when the focus is on storytelling, brand values, and audience trust.

3. Strategic Integration: Influencers as PR Allies

Forward-thinking PR professionals no longer view influencers as separate from traditional media—they view them as new-age media outlets.

Here's how PR teams strategically integrate influencers:

- Audience Alignment: Influencers are chosen based on their relevance to the target demographic and the trust they command within niche communities.
- Co-created Content: Instead of dictating scripts, PR teams collaborate with influencers to co-create content that feels authentic and resonates with their followers.
- Campaign Amplification: Influencers are often brought in to boost visibility for product launches, corporate initiatives, social causes, or brand narratives.
- Measurement of Success: PR professionals use engagement rates, sentiment analysis, and share of voice to track campaign success—not just vanity metrics like impressions.

This strategic alignment transforms influencers from ad channels into storytellers, helping brands forge deeper connections with audiences.

4. Credibility Through Influence—If Done Right

One of PR's core objectives is to build credibility. But can influencer marketing, often associated with sponsored content, achieve the same?

Yes—but with caveats. Influencer marketing builds credibility when it is authentic, transparent, and aligned with brand values.

Audiences are quick to spot inauthentic endorsements. However, when influencers genuinely believe in a product or message, their advocacy can be even more powerful than a traditional news article.

This is especially true with micro- and nano-influencers who is smaller. In most cases niche audiences often trust their recommendations more than mass media.

So, while influencer marketing doesn't guarantee credibility, when executed thoughtfully under a PR strategy, it can enhance a brand's trustworthiness and relatability.

5. Navigating the Blurred Lines in Client Strategies

The growing overlap between PR and influencer marketing has created a strategic grey area–especially in client communications. When presenting to clients, agencies must clarify how both disciplines work in tandem.

Here's how top agencies approach it:

- Define Each Channel: Clearly distinguish between earned, owned, and paid media in campaign strategies.
- Show the Synergy: Emphasize how influencer collaborations can reinforce PR messaging and extend reach.
- Present Unified Metrics: Use integrated dashboards that track media mentions, influencer engagement, sentiment, and conversions under one lens.
- Highlight Reputation Outcomes: Clients care about results–so focus on how influencer efforts contribute to reputation, awareness, and trust.

In pitches, successful agencies present influencer marketing not as a separate add-on, but as a core component of a modern, results-driven PR strategy.

Final Thoughts: The Future is Integrated

Influencers haven't replaced PR—they've expanded its possibilities. In today's landscape, where trust and authenticity drive consumer behaviour, influencers provide PR professionals with new ways to connect, inspire, and influence.

As digital platforms evolve and audiences grow more selective about what they consume, the most effective PR strategies will be those that embrace integration—uniting the credibility of traditional PR with the reach and relatability of influencers.

In this new era, PR has not just moved with the times—it has reshaped its identity. And influencers are not competitors—they're collaborators in the art of communication.

3.

Measuring What Matters: The Importance of PR Metrics

Public Relations (PR) is a critical function in shaping a brand's reputation, yet measuring its return on investment (ROI) remains a challenge. PR professionals and industry bodies continue to debate the best measurement metrics, but a universally accepted formula has yet to be established. Effective PR measurement is essential to justify budgets, demonstrate impact, and refine strategies for greater success. Without reliable measurement, PR efforts risk being undervalued and overlooked in the broader marketing mix.

A strong PR measurement framework allows organizations to:

- Identify what works and what doesn't in their PR strategies
- Align PR goals with broader business objectives
- Optimize resource allocation and maximize returns
- Prove the effectiveness of PR efforts to stakeholders

Key Aspects of PR Measurement

1. Available Measurement Metrics

There are various ways to measure PR effectiveness, ranging from traditional media coverage to more advanced digital analytics. Some common metrics include:

- **Media Impressions and Reach** – Gauging the extent of audience exposure
- **Sentiment Analysis** – Assessing whether coverage is positive, neutral, or negative
- **Share of Voice** – Comparing brand mentions against competitors
- **Website Traffic Generated from PR Activities** – Evaluating impact on digital engagement
- **Engagement on Digital and Social Media Platforms** – Measuring interactions such as likes, shares, and comments
- **Lead Generation and Conversion Rates** – Tracking the extent to which PR efforts translate into business leads

2. Industry Practices in Evaluating PR Campaigns

Different industries have adopted various evaluation models to assess PR success. Some organizations still rely on Advertising Value Equivalency (AVE), while others have moved towards data-driven models such as:

- **Barcelona Principles for PR evaluation** – A set of global standards focusing on qualitative and quantitative impact

- **Outcome-based Measurement Focused on Business Impact** – Tracking how PR contributes to sales, reputation, or customer loyalty
- **Media Quality Scoring and Message pull-through Analysis** – Evaluating how well key messages are conveyed in media coverage
- **Brand Sentiment Tracking** – Understanding how PR activities influence audience perceptions over time

3. Challenges in PR Measurement

Despite the advancements in PR measurement, several challenges persist:

- **Lack of Standardized Measurement Models** – PR success is often subjective and varies across industries
- **Attribution Issues** – Differentiating PR-driven impact from other marketing activities
- **Difficulty in Measuring Long-term Reputation impact** – Unlike digital marketing, PR outcomes may take months or years to manifest
- **Reliance on Outdated metrics like AVE** – Many companies still use AVE, despite its lack of accuracy in demonstrating true PR value

4. Credibility of PR Measurement Today

PR measurement faces scrutiny regarding its accuracy and relevance. The credibility of PR metrics depends on factors such as:

- **The Reliability of Media Monitoring Tools** – Ensuring accurate tracking of media mentions
- **The Correlation between PR efforts and Actual Business Outcomes** – Linking PR activities to measurable business goals
- **The Objectivity of Measurement Methodologies** – Avoiding bias in evaluation frameworks to improve credibility, organizations should:
- Use third-party media monitoring and analytics tools.
- Align PR measurement with key performance indicators (KPIs) tied to business success.
- Focus on qualitative aspects such as reputation enhancement and message effectiveness.

5. Best Practices in PR Measurement Internationally

Globally, PR measurement has evolved with best practices that emphasize tangible outcomes. Leading PR organizations recommend:

- Moving Away from AVE and Focusing on Engagement-driven Metrics – Measuring real influence rather than estimated ad costs
- Using AI-powered Analytics for Precise Audience Insights – Leveraging machine learning to assess PR effectiveness
- Aligning PR Goals with Broader Business Objectives – Ensuring PR efforts contribute to sales, reputation, and stakeholder trust

- Measuring Earned Media Value (EMV) – Assessing PR impact through engagement, media quality, and audience reach
- Adopting Integrated Analytics Platforms – Consolidating PR, social media, and web analytics for a holistic evaluation

6. Indian PR Bodies and Their Recommendations on PR Measurement

In India, PR bodies such as the Public Relations Consultants Association of India (PRCAI) and the Public Relations Society of India (PRSI) have been working towards standardized measurement frameworks. Key recommendations include:

- **Adoption of Global Measurement Standards** – Encouraging the industry to align with international best practices
- **Greater Integration of Digital Analytics in PR Evaluation** – Moving beyond traditional media monitoring to data-driven insights
- **Enhanced Transparency in Reporting PR Impact** – Using third-party verification and automated measurement tools
- **Stronger Focus on Stakeholder Engagement Metrics** – Assessing PR's role in investor relations, public affairs, and corporate social responsibility (CSR)
- **Encouraging Brands to Invest in Long-term Reputation Measurement** – Tracking brand sentiment, crisis management effectiveness, and thought leadership

Future of PR Measurement

As technology advances, PR measurement is expected to become even more data driven. Emerging trends include:

- **AI-driven Sentiment Analysis** – Automated tools that provide deeper insights into audience perceptions
- **Predictive Analytics** – Forecasting PR outcomes based on historical data
- **Blockchain for Media Verification** – Ensuring credibility and transparency in earned media valuation
- **Integration with CRM Systems** – Linking PR impact directly to customer relationship management and sales funnels

Conclusion

While PR measurement continues to evolve, the industry must work towards universally accepted standards that accurately reflect PR's role in influencing brand perception and business success. Organizations that embrace data-driven PR evaluation will be better positioned to optimize their strategies and demonstrate real ROI. PR professionals must continue to advocate for more sophisticated, transparent, and outcome-based measurement models to ensure PR's place as a critical business function.

4.

The Future of PR In India: A Promising Path for Brands and Professionals

The Evolution of PR and its Expanding Horizons

Public Relations (PR) in India is undergoing a significant transformation, driven by technological advancements, changing media landscapes, and evolving consumer expectations. The perception of PR has moved beyond mere publicity–it is now a critical component of brand building, reputation management, and crisis communication. In an era where news breaks at the drop of a hat and narratives shape consumer decisions, PR professionals are in greater demand than ever before.

Brands today rely on PR more than ever, not just for media coverage but to foster meaningful engagement with their audiences. Digital platforms, social media influencers, and AI-driven content strategies have redefined how PR operates. As a result, the industry is seeing exponential growth, creating new opportunities for professionals and agencies alike. This makes it an exciting time for young aspirants to explore the field and carve a niche in the industry.

Key Aspects Shaping the Future of PR in India

- **PR as a Pillar of Reputation Management:** A brand's reputation is one of its most valuable assets. PR plays a crucial role in building and maintaining this reputation through strategic communication, crisis management, and storytelling. Companies are increasingly investing in PR professionals who can craft compelling narratives, enhance brand credibility, and manage stakeholder relationships effectively. As the Indian market becomes more competitive, businesses are realizing that well-managed PR efforts can set them apart and create long-term trust among consumers.
- **Self-Belief and Confidence in PR Campaigns:** One of the essential qualities of a successful PR professional is self-belief. Managing a PR campaign requires resilience, creativity, and confidence to influence public perception. Whether it is media outreach, event management, or social media communication, PR specialists must trust their strategies and remain adaptable in a fast-paced environment. The ability to craft authentic and persuasive messaging determines how effectively a brand's story reaches its target audience.
- **The Role of AI, VR, and Emerging Technologies:** Technology is revolutionizing PR in ways never seen before. Artificial Intelligence (AI) is being used to analyse consumer sentiment, automate media monitoring, and

generate data-driven PR strategies. Virtual Reality (VR) is enhancing brand storytelling, providing immersive experiences that engage audiences at a deeper level. With these innovations, PR campaigns are becoming more precise, impactful, and measurable. Professionals who embrace AI-driven analytics and digital tools will have a competitive edge in the evolving PR landscape.

- **Promising Career Options in PR for Young Professionals:** The PR industry in India is growing rapidly, offering numerous career paths for aspiring professionals. With opportunities spanning corporate communications, digital PR, influencer marketing, crisis management, and government relations, young talents can find their niche based on their skills and interests. The demand for strategic communicators who can blend traditional PR methods with digital storytelling is on the rise. Those with expertise in media relations, content creation, and brand positioning will have ample opportunities in agencies, corporate firms, and start-ups alike.
- **The Need for More PR Institutions and Skill Development:** As the industry expands, there is a pressing need to develop specialized talent. India requires more institutions dedicated to PR education, training, and professional development. Upskilling programs, industry collaborations, and certification courses can bridge the talent gap and prepare professionals to meet evolving industry demands. Encouraging students and young professionals to pursue

formal training in PR will not only boost the quality of professionals entering the field but also contribute to the industry's long-term success.

Conclusion: A Golden Era for PR in India

The future of PR in India is promising, with technology, creativity, and strategy at its core. As brands continue to recognize the power of PR in shaping their identity and maintaining public trust, the demand for skilled professionals will only rise. Young aspirants entering the field have a world of opportunities ahead, provided they stay adaptable, innovative, and committed to continuous learning. With the right mix of expertise and passion, PR professionals can play a transformative role in shaping narratives, influencing perceptions, and building brands that stand the test of time.

Acknowledgements

Over the years, my journey as a writer has been one of continuous learning, growth, and evolution. It all began in 2006 when my very first article was published in *The Hindu Business Line*. I still remember the mix of excitement and nervousness I felt seeing my work in print for the first time. That milestone was the start of a path that has brought me immense fulfilment and countless opportunities.

Writing on subjects close to my heart—Advertising, Marketing, and Public Relations—has been both a passion and a privilege. These areas have constantly challenged me to stay curious, updated, and connected with an ever-changing industry. However, as time went on, I realized that to truly engage and serve my audience, I needed to broaden my scope. Today, I write about a wide range of topics that are relevant, practical, and digestible for readers who want insights they can immediately apply or relate to.

This journey has not been without its challenges. There were moments of self-doubt, writer's block, and the pressure to stay relevant in a fast-paced media landscape. But every setback was a lesson that pushed me to refine my craft, deepen my understanding, and find my authentic voice.

I want to take this moment to express my sincere gratitude to the platforms that believed in me and gave me the space to share my stories. Adgully, Afaqs, Reputation Today, Medianews4u and Best Media Info, have been more than just publication channels

—they have been partners in my journey, allowing me to reach a wider audience and connect with readers and industry professionals alike.

Equally, if not more importantly, I owe a heartfelt thanks to the many industry leaders, experts, and visionaries who have generously shared their time, insights, and perspectives with me. Your willingness to collaborate and open up has not only enriched my articles but has also deepened my own understanding of this dynamic field. Your support has been invaluable, and I am truly grateful for the trust and relationship we have built.

As I look ahead, I remain committed to growing as a writer and storyteller—always learning, listening, and striving to offer content that informs, inspires, and resonates with my audience. Thank you for being part of this journey with me.